Shear Flow Turbulence

Anna Heiður Oddsdóttir

Copyright

Copyright © 2024, Anna Heiður Oddsdóttir
All rights reserved.

The poems and design of this book may not be reproduced, stored in a retrieval system, or transmitted in any form or by any means—electronic, mechanical, photocopying, recording, or otherwise—without prior written permission from the author, except for brief quotations used in reviews or critical articles.

All illustrations in this book are sourced from Wikimedia or created with AI. See credits and usage guidelines at the end.

This book is a work of original creative expression. Any resemblance to real persons, living or dead, events, or locations is purely coincidental.

Dedication

To my parents, Margrét and Oddur, who gave me the gift of life and nurtured my growth. They instilled in me a love for thinking, reading and writing.

To my sister, Embla, whose fresh perspective and curiosity are a wellspring of ideas. Her insights have been invaluable throughout this journey.

To our children, Alex, Fjóna and Robert, the lifeblood of our existence. Their compassion, and deep care for others bring hope for a brighter, kinder future. If everyone shared their spirit, the world would be a better place.

To my husband and son, Mike and Justin, who are no longer with us but whose presence is felt every day in our lives and hearts.

To my dog Isidora, who carries on the legacy of her cherished sister Melkorka. She reminds me daily that, while writing poetry may be a noble pursuit, lavishing attention and treats is equally vital.

To Luna, Zorak, and all those resting in Öskjuhlíð, whose memories continue to live in our hearts.

To my friend, Gurpreet, a steadfast supporter who always encourages my writing.

Finally, to you — the reader and co-creator. May this book prove worthy of your time and imagination.

About Author

I was born and raised in Iceland, a land of stark contrasts, famously known as 'The Land of Fire and Ice.' These contrasts resonate deeply within my mind and soul. My wonderful family is of utmost importance to me, shaping my perspectives and grounding my life. After spending a few years in Los Angeles, California, where I studied anthropology, linguistics, and various aspects of filmmaking at UCLA, I returned to Iceland. I worked at the National Broadcasting Service for many years as a producer and director, contributing to news programs and documentaries.

Some years ago, a significant life event inspired me to begin writing poetry, though I will spare you the details. Now, I live in the north of Iceland, where I continue to explore and express my thoughts and emotions through poetry. My hope is that these poems resonate with you. If even one finds a place in your heart, I will consider myself a fortunate poet.

Credits

This book was expertly designed and formatted by Jooneyd Raza, who handled formatting and layout.

Jooneyd Raza is a seasoned professional in the field of book design and formatting. With over 5 years of experience, Jooneyd has assisted more than 1,000 clients worldwide in preparing their works for self-publishing.

In addition to providing services to authors globally, Jooneyd has also successfully published his own books on Amazon Kindle Direct Publishing (KDP).

For inquiries or to discuss how Jooneyd can help with your book project, please reach out via email at: **jooneydraza@gmail.com**

Table of Contents

On the Run 1

The Quiet Apocalypse 3

Still Drowning 6

Crossing the Chasm 10

Resurgence 13

The Heart of Their Courage 15

The Sheer Cliff 18

The Grocery Gauntlet 21

Flight of Fear 24

Realms Surpassing Reason 27

Nightshift, August 1968 30

Beyond the Map 33

Movements and Modulations 35

Boxes Black and Gold 38

Eternal Spring 40

Relentless Rhythm 42

Woven Through 45

Hideaway 49

Hidden Fury 53

New Neighbours 55

The Race Against Silence 57

The Unyielding Hour 60

Bedrock of Change 63
Poetry in Motion 65
Burgers and Fries 68
Misericorde 70
Veil of Kindness 72
Violations 74
Alicorn 77
Strength From Struggle 79

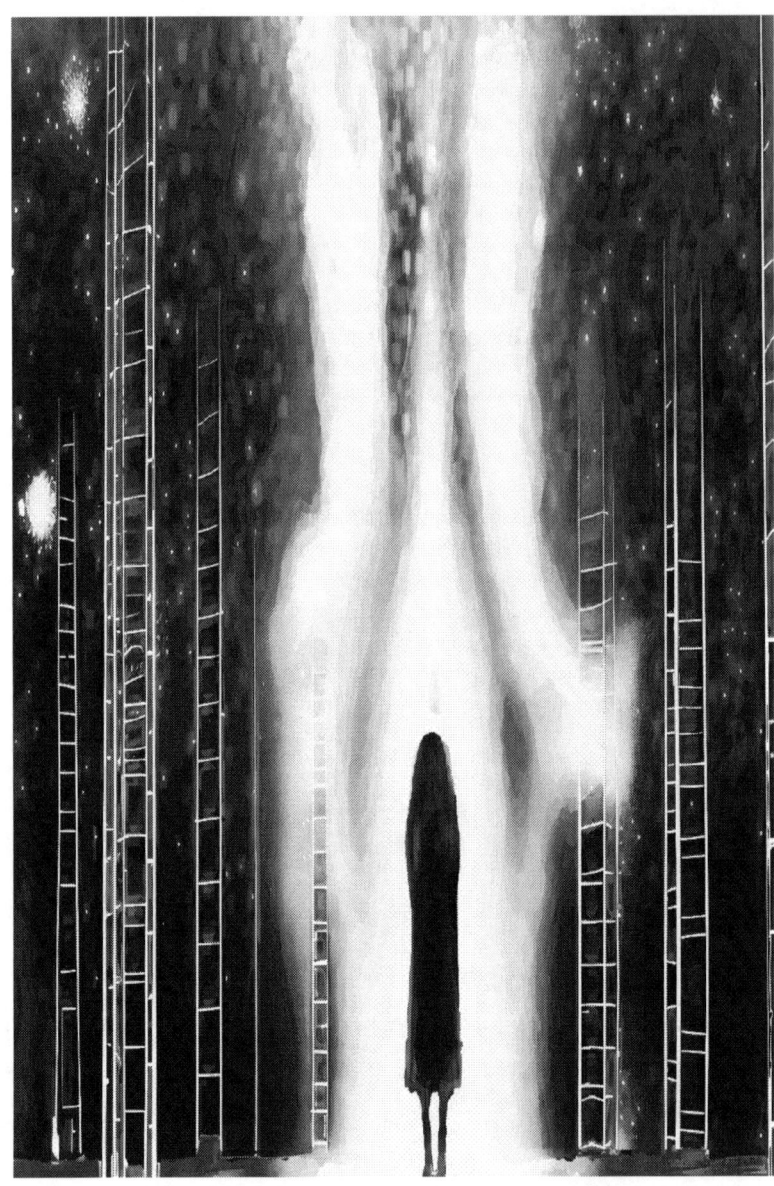

On the Run

Five minutes ago, I had an idea,
I daresay it was a good one.
Now it's slipped away.

Just like that,
it wandered deep
into the recesses of my mind.
I know it's still there, somewhere.

The more I try to retrieve it, the faster it flees,
like a shadow fading with the light.

I gaze out the window,
watching withered leaves twirl in the wind,
each one a moment drifting away.

Perhaps it will resurface,
in five minutes or five years, or maybe it's lost forever,
like countless instants we fail to grasp.

Wait! — a vague recollection stirs.
It had something to do with
the fleeting nature of time, the fragility of life,
and the certainty of endings.

Thoughts, like autumn leaves,
pirouette briefly in the breeze
before they crumble —
a reminder that everything,
no matter how vibrant, is ephemeral.

As they scatter, these fragments reside
in the spaces between,
a dance of reflection and memory, suggesting
that some truths endure, even if our steps falter.

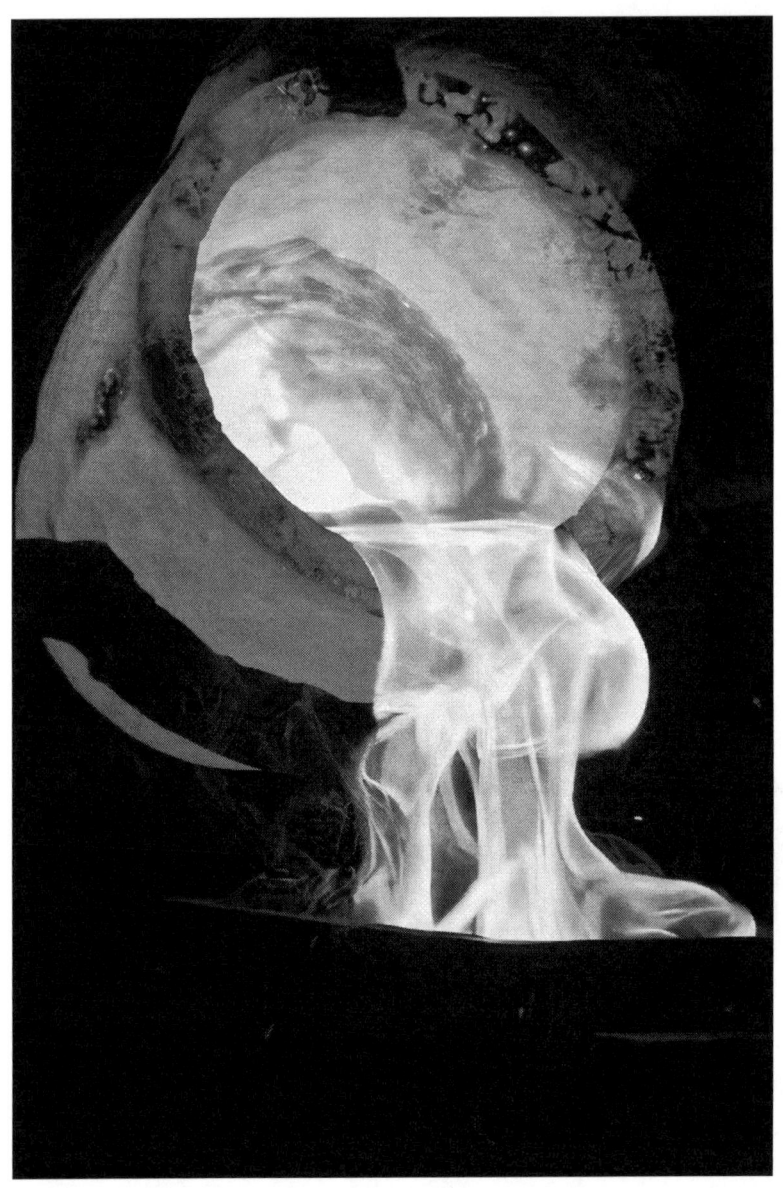

The Quiet Apocalypse

She was lured by a future,
glinting like gold at rainbow's end.

But she turned away —
became a child behind factory doors,
hands worn raw, feeding the greed of machines
that devoured hours and breath.

A sparrow cowering beneath the hawk's shadow,
she watched iron serpents hiss,
erasing miles, carrying souls,
leaving only echoes behind.

She felt the world tighten its grip,
like an octopus ensnared in steel jaws,
her struggle growing desperate,
as walls rose high around her,
burying dreams once cradled for her child.
Dread was the mortar, binding every cold brick.

She bore the burden of a father,
heart weighed down with unspoken words,
learning to hide tenderness
beneath armor forged by expectation,
his love trapped within pride's prison.

Dragged like a dog by heavy chains
into the ring of teeth,
where the crowd's roar devoured the last of mercy.
And the force of cruelty grew, unrelenting,
as she was pulled further from herself.

Like a chicken, clipped and torn,
pressed into wire-bound confines,
her life measured in weight,
her heartbeats uncounted.

Every ounce of resistance diminished,
until she was nothing
but another product to be consumed.

She became the goose, force-fed in darkness,
her swollen liver a delicacy
for the indifferent.

She was told to bend, to break,
and mute what made her whole,
locked in a place
that fears what it cannot hold.

She starved while the banquet spilled over,
just a turn away.

In despair's crucible,
her sorrow melted, reshaped,
transforming into empathy.

We build our towers of glass,
watch the earth splinter beneath,
the hidden catastrophe
lurking at our feet.

Still, we anchor ourselves
to lonely islands,
eyes closed to those adrift,
reaching for shores
we never meant to share.

To be human is to feel,
but we harden — stone beneath our skin,
deaf to whispers of suffering,
until indifference shatters the silence,
and the quiet apocalypse
speaks louder than anything else.

Still Drowning

*One night, two tragedies at sea: A crowded refugee boat
seeking sanctuary capsizes in the Mediterranean;
A submersible, carrying thrill-seekers to explore the Titanic's
wreckage, plunges to its doom.*

We embarked at dawn's first light,
hearts woven with fragile dreams,
bound for horizons unknown.
An ocean away, a dive commences —
five souls enclosed in steel and glass,
their venture fuelled by excitement,
a chosen surrender to the abyss.

As night cloaked the world in shadow,
the sea turned to chaos —
the promise of safety,
a cruel illusion
crafted by those who bartered lives for gold.

Amid hundreds, we fought the tempest,
our vessel overwhelmed,
my boy and his mother, claimed by merciless waves,
her delicate fingers slipping from my desperate grasp,
two lives vanished into the unfathomable dark.

Simultaneously, the submersible, once a sanctuary,
becomes an iron grave.
Silent screams swallowed by the depths,
an avoidable misadventure unfolds.

Headlines emerge,
printed with the ink of a disaster born from thrill,
not from necessity.

I saw my daughter — my joy —
yield to the current,
her misplaced trust pulsing in my veins.
Her cries reverberate through the core of my being,
her face etched with fear remains,
eyes reflecting the moon,
fading into the consuming blue.

Yet I see her still — in the crest of each wave,
every subtle disturbance,
imprinted on the ocean's endless canvas,
an ache that cannot be drowned.

The current unwavering, I am but a leaf,
my lungs plead for air,
my chest pounding a frantic rhythm,
each breath a fervent plea, a silent struggle.

The waves cradle me now,
their unwelcome embrace tightens.
In the solitude of my final moments,
I join them — my family, taken by the Aegean.

Within the throes of such immense loss,
we sway between the drowned
and those still drowning.

Our shared tale fragments
into solitary chapters,
a microcosm of a crisis too vast,
too profound.

The world mourns the privileged five,
their names immortalized
in newsprint and collective tears.
Yet hundreds of us,
engulfed by the ocean's vastness,
drift as faceless footnotes,
in the annals of whispered disasters.

A new day dawns, revealing stark divides —
a sunken luxury explored, a vessel submerged,
rescue efforts ignited for some,
while we stay unseen, unheard,
our stories blending with the quiet hum
of undisturbed waters.

We are mere traces of those who journeyed before,
silenced warnings to those
yet to brave the treacherous sea.

Still drowning — yesterday, today, tomorrow —
in unrelenting tides,
and the recesses of selective memory.

Crossing the Chasm

Suspended high above the rushing stream
of cars, like ants upon the road below,
a sudden wave of vertigo strikes.

My legs give way, I collapse.
Beside me, sister stifles a chuckle, yet
her eyes betray concern as I,
on all fours, begin to creep forward.

The concrete, cold and unforgiving, scrapes
my hands but offers stability.
Around me, strangers stare, faces mixed
with pity and amusement
as I crawl.

The hum of engines,
a rising cacophony,
intertwines with my racing heart.
I sense the vast expanse beneath, the dizzying height,
sticking to the structure —
more like cling wrap on a leftover
than a nimble mountain goat.

The depth below spins, a swirling chasm,
and with every move, I feel like I'm drifting,
weightless, untethered.

I grip the cold edge of the bridge,
its rough surface the only solid thing,
the only anchor,
holding me against the pull of the void.

Determined, every movement,
each trembling breath, a victory.
My sister guides me through
the chaos I've created, hand on shoulder,
her touch a gentle reassurance,
grounding.

The wind whips past, tugging at my clothes,
a stark reminder of the open air.
Still, I press on, stubborn, persistent,
refusing to let fear hinder my path.

As I approach the end, panic's clasp
loosens, my breathing steadies,
calm returning.
I rise to my feet,
the world less daunting now,
sister's encouragement,
my stabilizing force.

Afterwards, I stand humbled, yet proud,
no longer a prisoner to dread.
The bridge,
once a symbol of terror,
now a monument to triumph
over fear.

Resurgence

In winter's unforgiving grasp,
a startling burst of red.
Once faded, the rose regains its hue,
crimson petals, velvet and luminous,
against the snow's cold shroud.

Rising, reclaiming, it discovers
a tranquil strength above the storm-swept earth,
embracing raw resilience.

A helix of renewal spirals upward,
forever turning, always returning,
to the core of nature's pulse.
Tendrils foretell unfolding leaves
as soil begins to thaw,
the first delicate touch of spring.

Time and time again,
the rose bowed its head,
seeking solace in the intoxicating ground,
until it chose to bloom once more,
its vibrant colour restored.

A hummingbird hovers nearby,
drawn to the sublime transformation,
bearing witness to the power
of perseverance and resolve.

Heralding rebirth,
its presence a reminder
that even in the darkest times,
hope nurtures hope,
and life breaks through.

The Heart of Their Courage

Between winter's frosted claws,
two roses, vibrant and bold,
blossom above the snow,
midnight purple with evergreen dots.

Together they cast a glow
across the icy plain,
little moons becoming golden suns.

Baring its teeth, the cold wind roars,
challenging their delicate existence.
They shiver and sway but persevere,
quietly forging a pact to survive.

Their past a waltz across hidden landmines,
now each rose holds its ground,
fragrant flames illuminating
the dim, deep night,
an expression of tenacity,
soft but unyielding,
they bode an early spring.

Whispers float on the frost's breath,
memories of battles fought.
Warriors wounded in action,
their armour worn thin,
the roses remain wellsprings of warmth,
twin testimonies that even in the harshest hours,
hope stays, life continues.

A passing traveller halts,
his breath crystallizing in the crisp air.
Enchanted by the unexpected blooms,
he reflects on nature's indomitable power —
its potential to astonish and inspire.

His spirit, sapped and worn
from hardships weathered and scars unseen,
finds comfort in their fortitude.
Reminded of his own struggles,
their presence soothes his aching soul,
brightening the dark path.

Emerging from the innermost reaches
of splitting pain and irretrievable loss,
undernourished in barren soil,
daughters of wintry fields arise,
reaching out to the world.

Roots entwined, they mature together,
fusing vigour and grace,
forging an enduring bond,
a tale of shared strength.

The Sheer Cliff

Confined to the wheelchair since morning light,
the sun entices me through the glass,
a distant reminder of freedom.

Won't be going out today, one arm useless,
steering rod broken, they promised to fix it by noon.
But here I remain, trapped.
Left alone with my thoughts and needs,
really must pee and such,
the caregiver is late again,
as if my time doesn't matter.
I will have to let it go.

The clock strikes six.
I am mired in waste, my skin itching,
the stench makes me gag every time.

A mountaineer grounded,
living under a low roof,
traversing garden paths to nowhere.

I look out the kitchen window.
Blue in the distance, out of reach,
the mountain, my only friend.

With sharp peaks, sheer cliffs
and gentle slopes,
how magnificent its beauty.
My hand caressed its face,
hard yet soft at once
and I was touched in return.

In my forced idleness
I struggle to express
my boundless love for it.

My pen poised over a blank page
but the words elude me,
lost in the vastness of the mountain's splendour.

It is getting dark.
My reflection alone in the kitchen window,
I pity what I see there,
a pale version of the self I used to know,
my spirit bound, unable to ascend.

Despair becomes resolve
as I fix my eyes on a knife by the sink.
I reach for it with trembling fingers.

Then hold it firmly, ready to sever ties,
longing for release,
in its keen point and smooth edge.

Do I dare climb the sheer cliff, never to come back?

The Grocery Gauntlet

Hellbent I enter the supermarket's realm,
a world of vivid hues and staggering choices,
profusion of aisles, shelves packed to the brim.

Focus slips, elusive as sand —
I grasp the cart, my anchor,
list clutched tight, a lifeline in the maze.
A mind untethered, navigating unseen hurdles,
racing thoughts refuse to be restrained.
Inwardly I recite, a grounding mantra:

Whatever I do, I must not forget the bread.

Sensory flash floods, drowning in a sea of options.
My hyperfocus ignited, each decision
another twist in the labyrinth.
With every turn, tension mounts,
a tide I cannot hold back.
Urgency to leave thrums in my veins.

In the produce section, a fleeting moment of calm —
I breathe, centring scattered thoughts,
yet restless energy rears,
like a wild horse, untamed and unwilling to halt,
as it rushes me forward.

Then it dawns on me, realization sharp and clear,
I can't see any tomatoes!
How can there be no tomatoes?

WHY ARE THERE NO TOMATOES?

Anxiety swells, seesawing on panic's edge,
but at last, I spot them — misplaced.
The section rearranged, unnecessary change —
my constant foe.

Clock ticks, life's relentless march,
glancing at my list, items left behind,
forgetful as I dart through the maze.
Inwardly, I recite the grounding mantra:

Whatever I do, I must remember the bread.

My life, a perpetual fray
between impulse and concentration,
the market, a microcosm, a test of mettle.

Gathering strength,
I push on with determination,
a warrior on a mundane battleground.

Through the labyrinth I weave and sway,
a chaotic twirl in pursuit of sustenance.
Reaching the checkout, a sense of triumph.
Despite the whirlwind, my tornado still sleeps.

Inwardly, I recite a final refrain:

Whatever I did, I did not forget the bread.

Flight of Fear

I step aboard, shadowed by a premonition,
the ghost of dread trailing close behind,
hands tremble, heart gallops,
as I flop into my seat.

Anxiety builds, my restless hands
fidget and shift,
eyes fixed on the window —
the world dissolves.

The captain's voice, steady and calm,
promises good conditions, favourable weather,
a pleasant flight ahead —
his words jinx the still air,
and in my mind, a dark omen takes root.

"Don't let fear control you," they say,
"Flying is the safest way to travel."
Yet unease seeps in,
a shiver that burrows deep.

Hours pass, but my tension remains,
a presence at my side, persistent,
as if fate itself tests my resolve.

My thoughts circle back
to the odds I've learned by heart:
1 in 11 million — the risk is small, they assure me,
but still, I am one.

Suddenly it begins —
the descent I've dreaded.
Turmoil erupts, the once calm cabin now a tempest.
Nervous murmurs spread like wildfire,
wide eyes dart, hands clutching armrests.
Survival hangs in a delicate balance.

Children cry, bewildered gazes
locked on their parents,
who hold them tight,
their soothing words muffled by fear.

The captain's voice, strained and desperate,
informs us of our fate.
Hope flickers and fades,
as flight attendants, masks frayed,
scramble to calm the storm around us.

In the midst of mayhem, I find
empathy swelling within,
our shared struggle binds us,
and for once, I am not alone in my fear.

As we steel ourselves
against certain collision with ground or sea,
a collective courage blooms.

Suddenly, absurdity grips me —
so many "ones" on this doomed plane,
the statistics seem hollow now.

Our fates are entwined, an unspoken bond.
We plummet toward the destiny
I have already imagined,
many times over.

Realms Surpassing Reason

Feathered moons entangle in silken skies,
the unknown drifts like fractured dreams.
Laughter ripples, shatters —
ponds of scattered stars.

Neon rivers, serpents of light,
coil, splinter, disperse into night.

Universes unfold, crumble, reform —
limitless and unbound.
Shadows glide, then vanish —
phantom echoes in a silent ballet.

Sun sets in the east, reappears in the west,
time loops upon itself, without end,
clocks reverse, stutter, fade.

Golden rays flicker,
silhouettes swoon,
chaos choreographed in cosmic rhythm.
Twisted nights,
labyrinthine marvels,
fearless wandering through the unseen.

Sands shift, oceans churn — flux and fracture,
crystal flames blaze, luminous currents flow
backward, upward, to nowhere.

Words weave within the mind's loom,
a baffling paradox, riddles unvoiced.

Lifted roots sway, suspended in the sky.
Gravity's forgotten pull as water ascends,
logic unspools, disintegrates,
tapestries of reality unravel,
threads of reason fray.

A teacup defies,
dances with tidal waves,
a tree sprouts from cold stone,
laughing at the earth.

Passengers slide on derailed trains,
alone yet together,
ruptured but whole,
journeying to nowhere.

Moons liquefy into molten amber,
solar flares, a choir of fire —
sing their celestial secrets.

The universal pulse of chaos and desire,
a mantra, a madness,
an existence entire.

Dreamscapes bewilder,
fragmented minds soar,
fantasy unfurls — realms boundless and wild.
Fear murmurs from obscure voids,
beauty fleeting, glimmers, dims —
an ephemeral charm.

Strange and wondrous,
a world half-formed,
an untamed voyage, an uncharted path.
Awe trembles within the heart,
changed, reclaimed, eternally renewed —
forgotten and remembered.

Clock chimes twice,
a heartbeat's echo,
returning, dissolving, with knowing eyes.
Memories linger, unreal, surreal,
deep within the soul —
an obscured truth revealed,
then lost again.

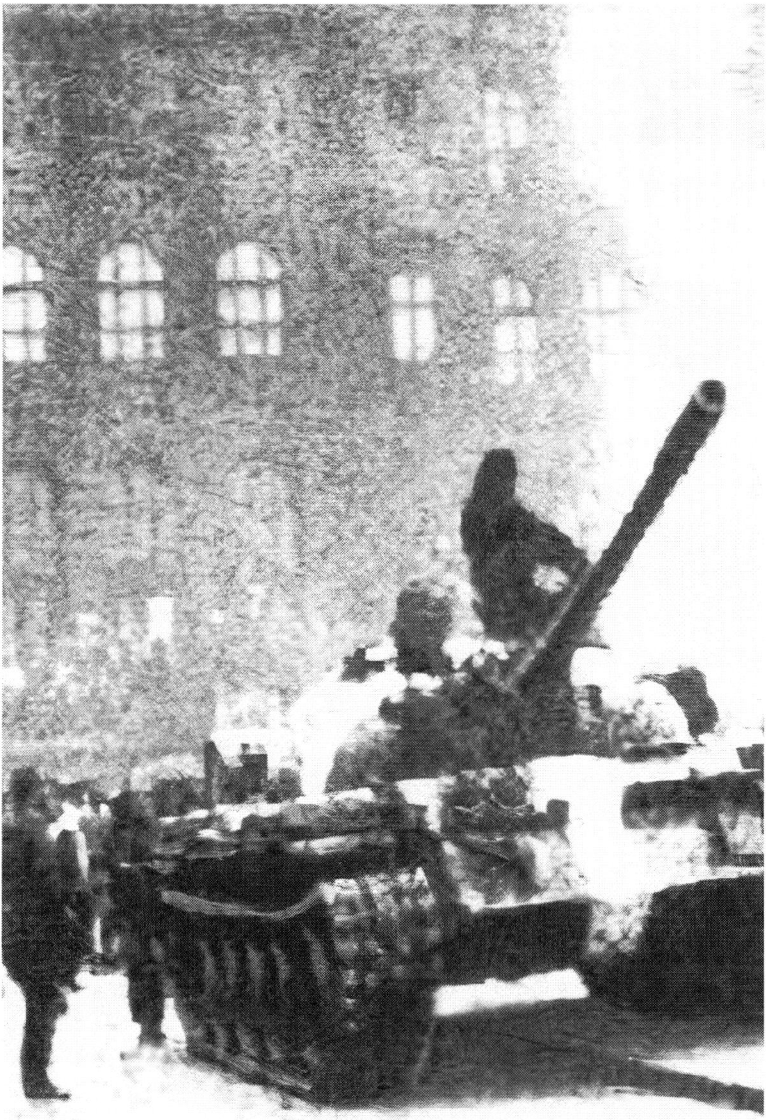

Nightshift, August 1968

At midnight, the BBC crackled to life —
Warsaw Pact forces rolled through the streets,
extinguishing the Prague Spring,
that brief, fragile bloom of possibility.
The newsroom buzzed
with the weight of dark bulletins,
and my mother, during late shift,
typed the world's sorrow
in hurried strokes.

Tanks ravaged Czechoslovakia,
crushing voices under their treads,
and in the depths of darkness,
the Cold War turned colder still.
History unravelled, lives were lost —
for a dream of liberty,
wrecked under steel and fear.

The printing presses ran by morning;
paper in hand, she stumbled home,
exhausted, eyes hollow,
with grief pressing down,
heavy as stone,
for a city locked in silence,
for the fallen she'd never met.

I was small, tugging at her skirt,
my scraped knee, raw and red,
aching with childish urgency,
my cries drowned out
by the headlines.
She said it wasn't serious —
right, of course,
but how I wanted her to see me.

Years later, now I understand.
The blow that shattered hope
broke something in her, too,
already fractured by early losses,
leaving no sense of safety or belonging.
And the hardness I resented then,
I now carry in my bones.
And my knee, long healed,
barely bled.

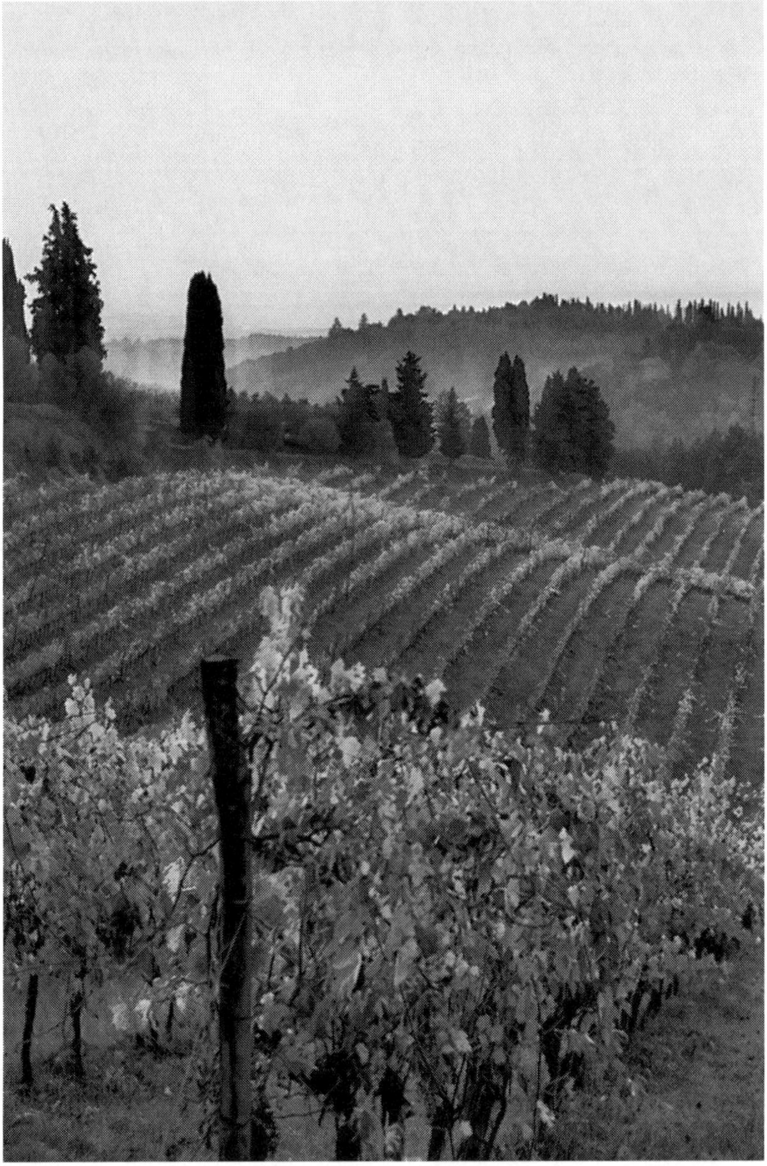

Beyond the Map

Our destination,
a vision of Siena,
bathed in Tuscany's liquid gold.

Your gift to me,
a memory of pure beauty.
Though how you recall it
and what I imagine,
never having been there,
may never meet.

Caught in a rainstorm,
we lose our way, take a wrong turn —
as often happens,
struggling to connect.
Flooded roads, hard to navigate.

We find ourselves en route to Rome,
pause to consult the maps,
realizing that the Siena
held in your recollection
isn't there.

Yet, amid the downpour,
we uncover something more profound;
time shared, filled with
surprises and adventure,
lighting on joy in the experience itself.

Though we wander
and sometimes fail to keep direction,
this journey together
charts a course through the maze of our love,
still glowing in Tuscany's golden light.

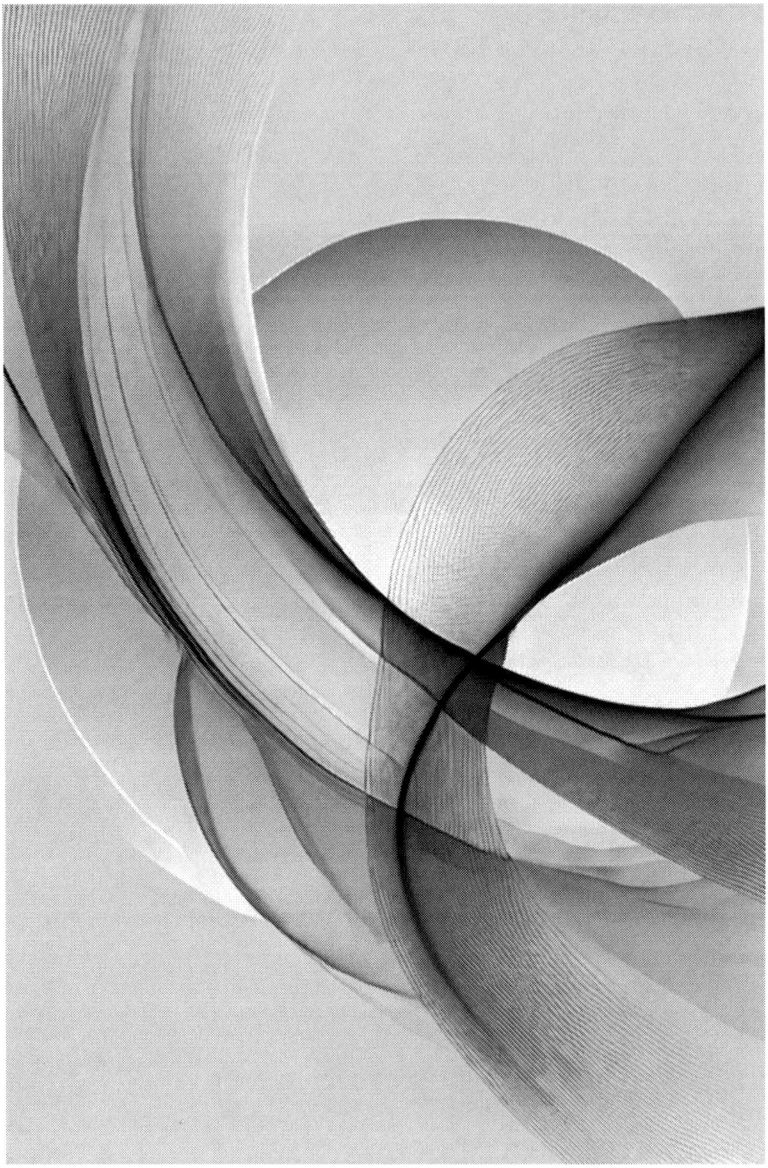

Movements and Modulations

Shadows pool in the evening's hold,
muted hues of fading echoes.
The day's murmurs are soft and spent,
diminishing volumes, resting serenely.
Moonlight sculpts the silence into form,
symphonic structures shaping space with song.
Stars thread a faint glow,
timbres delicate as high-pitched tones.

Dawn stirs, a slow unfurling calm,
a gradual crescendo — the start of a phrase.
Birdsong spills into the stillness, a fluid warmth,
a musical line emerging from quiet.

Morning breaks, painting the sky with breath,
a blend of colours in major key brightness.
Each moment a brushstroke, each sound a path,
flowing freedom, harmonic exploration.

Rivers trace melodies beneath the surface,
underlying bass lines, supportive undertones.
Light dances on water —
a luminous mirage,
syncopation in the play of gleam and shadow.

The world awakens, a canvas of motion,
polyphonic textures, multiple voices.
The sun's arc, a steady beat of energy,
a rhythm constant yet ever varied.

It moves with purpose, an animated dance,
allegro pace, lively interplay.
Themes weave through the fabric of afternoon,
counterpoint in complex layering.

Stories unfold in the warmth of daylight,
thematic development, evolving motifs.
Life's intricate tapestry, rich and abundant,
fortissimo — a lush fullness of sound.

Evening descends with a mellowing touch,
decrescendo — a return to subtler dynamics.
The day's rhythm slows, a gentle retreat,
ritardando before the final cadence.
Night comes to cradle the earth,
reverting to tonic, a resolution.
Dreams hover like whispers in the air,
a lingering finale — the enduring last note.

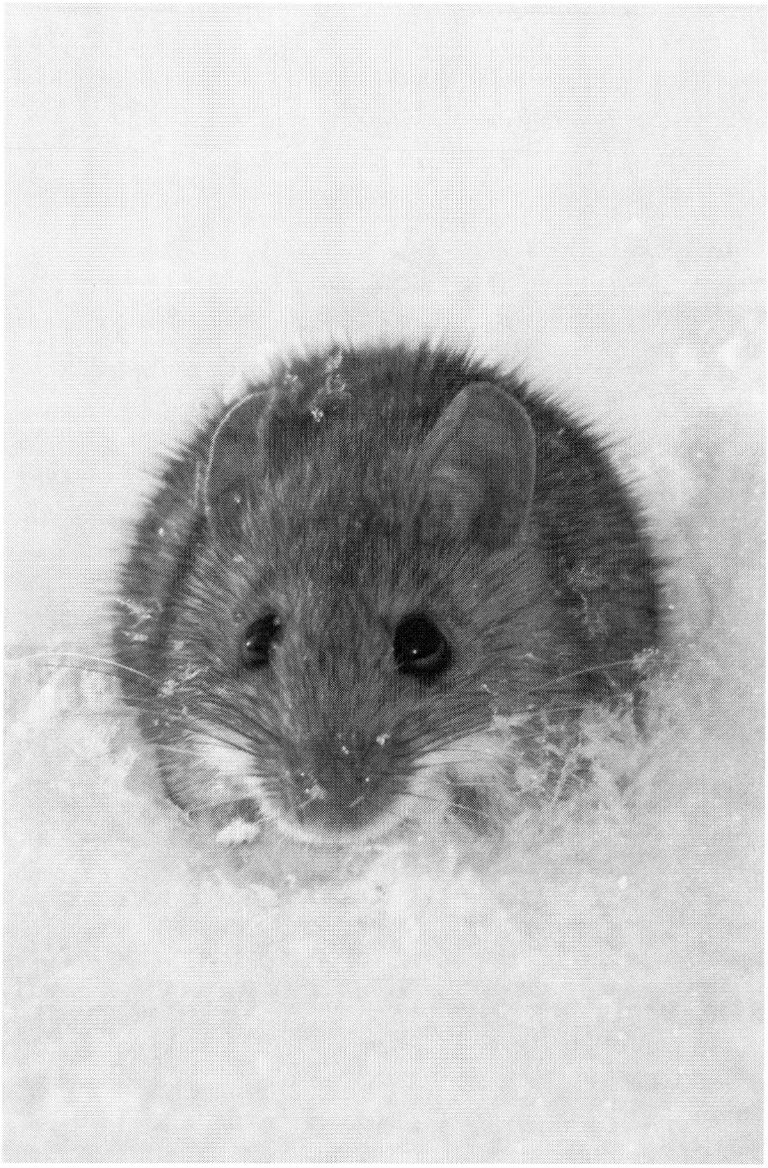

Boxes Black and Gold

Tiny and tender,
a beauty beyond words,
you lay on the veranda,
slender legs outstretched,
paws clenched against the storm.

Were you hoping, in vain,
for someone to let you in?
Did you perhaps swallow poison
from one of those black boxes
surrounding the warmth of this house?

My body trembles —
yours remains perfectly still.
Eyes dark brown, you shed no tears,
I cry more than I have in years.

For a little mouse,
left to wither
in the heart of winter,
for mortal creatures everywhere,
all who live and die,
never knowing why.
Questioning the purpose, while time slips by.

I place your body in a gilded box,
beneath the shelter of a bare tree.
I wonder —
Was it fear that kept you still?

Wait! Might you still be alive?
Hasten to unearth, hoping for rebirth,
remove the lid, ever so gently —
only to find, you have truly departed.

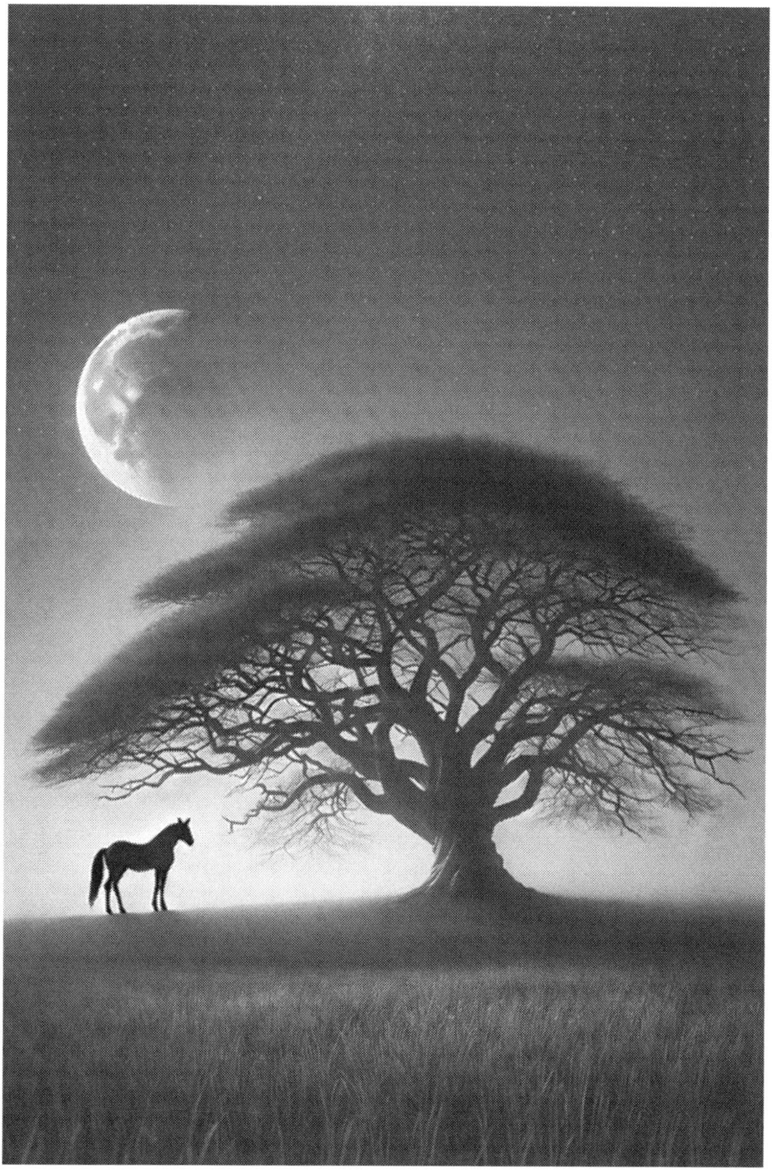

Eternal Spring

Remember the child who died so young,
so long ago,
and the infant star in the indigo sky,
born on that fateful night,
guiding me still with its light.

Shining steadily brighter,
growing with widening horizons,
that star has stayed with me ever since,
as has the warmth of your voice,
giving questions to all answers.

When I sleep too soundly,
the soft touch of your hand
on my tender cheek
awakens me gently from dreams.

But when shadows loom, I take the reins,
facing the beastly quartet of horsemen —
I ride my valiant steed, your gift to me,
its carved head held high,
wooden mane swirling,
single leg barely touching the ground.

While I ride with this steadfast companion,
I still feel your quiet strength beside me,
my constant compass through the dark.

One day, I will find you in the shade,
beneath the tree of life,
by love's eternal spring,
where the light of newborn stars
illuminates our journey's end
and the beginning of something timeless.

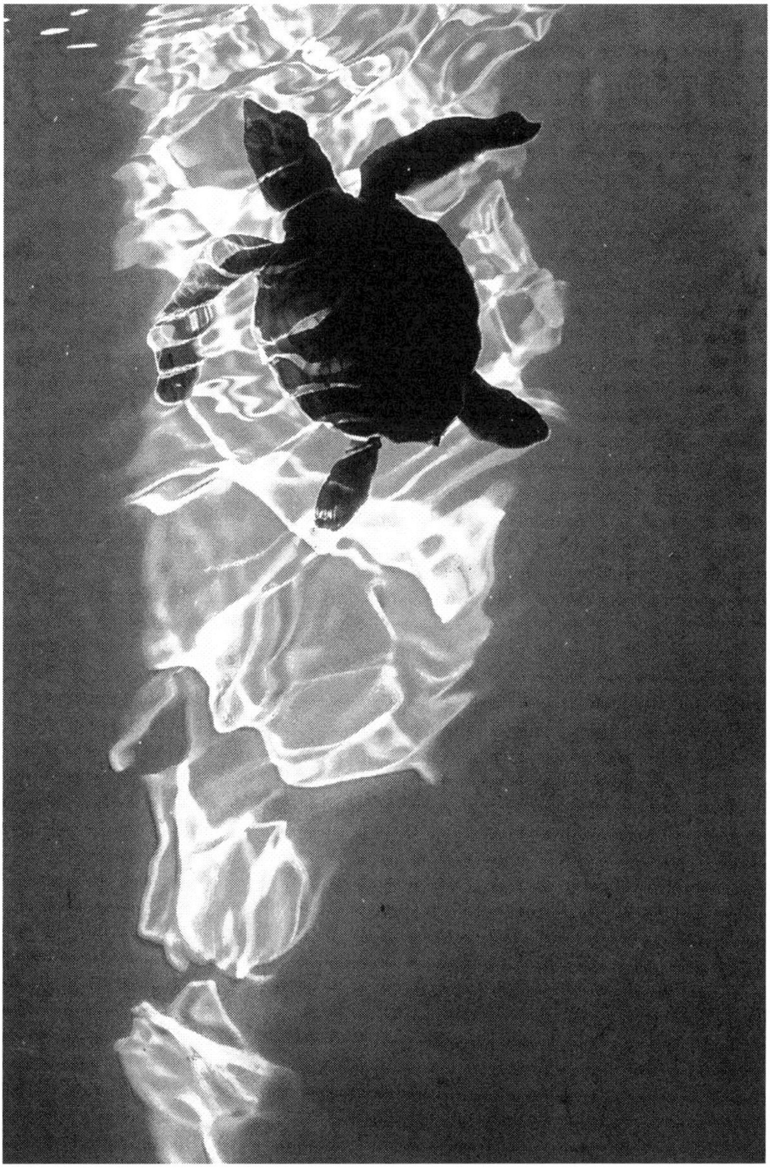

Relentless Rhythm

Under the moon's silvered eye,
a fragile being, no larger than a child's palm,
emerges, destined to navigate
the sands of time.

One among countless siblings,
a beat in nature's persistent pulse.

Born to strive against all odds,
hatchlings forge a path
across the treacherous shore,
their venture molded by unseen forces —
the ceaseless ebb and flow.

Waves crash, winds bite,
fear and determination etched
on their tiny faces.
Each step a trial, lungs burning with effort;
muscles straining against the elements.

Along a starlit beach,
guided by ancient instincts,
a lone hatchling glimmers in the night.

Barely evading a seagull's strike,
it presses forward, relentless,
as though the struggle itself
is woven into its purpose.

At the water's edge,
ghost crabs and predators prowl,
their shadows threatening with every step.

The young turtle, balancing
on a narrow margin, is caught
between survival and demise.

And there, at the boundary of the open sea,
its journey reaches a fateful close,
beyond the grasp of safety,
a brief yet valiant struggle,
now fading into memory.

The rhythm of existence, ever present.

Yet, beneath the same pale moon,
a sibling follows the perilous course,
its flippers defying the clutch
of shadowy hunters.

Through shifting ground,
it slips into the waiting sea,
escaping the precipice of danger
and plunging into mysterious waters.

A spark that eluded death,
it swims toward an unwritten future,
to compose a melody long and enduring,
a note lasting centuries
within the ocean's grand symphony.

44

Woven Through

We're at it again, the three of us,
words unravelling
like old yarn
tangled in the mundane.

It could be anything —
a small complaint,
or nothing at all.
You know us;
debates spinning without cease.

Voices rise like steam from a kettle,
clashing and blending
in the morning's warmth.

My husband crosses his arms,
"You're missing the point —
it's just practical.
You shouldn't leave lights on all night."

Our son smiles, nudging me playfully.
"I don't know, Dad.
Mom may have a point.
Leaving the lights on makes it seem
like someone's awake —
keeps away the unsavory types."

I raise an eyebrow, amused.
"Maybe I'm just keeping watch."
He chuckles.
"We've got it covered,"
teasing with youthful ease.
I shake my head,
"Oh, come on —
that's easy for you to say."

The air thickens,
familiar comfort slipping away.
"What makes it easy?"
you both ask,
heads tilting together,
a silent chorus.

The room softens,
as if anticipating my sorrow.
I hesitate,
unsure if I want to know.
Silence presses against me,
a heavy tapestry woven with memories.

Empty chairs sit
in their eternal vigil.
Expecting you to speak,
I sigh.
"Because... you're not here, are you?"

There are days when I try to let go —
but then I hear your laughter in the walls,
and my grip hardens again.
How could I move on without you,
when you greet me
at every corner of my day?

Grief sits on the shelves
like an old scar,
so deep it never disappears.
Sometimes I leave it untouched,
reluctant to sift through cobwebs
laden with pain.

Loss lingers in the dust
on books we never open.
You've been away so long,
yet somehow, you remain.

Every so often, I awake
to the scent of your coffee,
sunlight catching in your long, grey hair,
a half-smile as you pour,
waiting for me to speak.

How many mornings did I take for granted,
thinking there would always be more?

And my son —
it seemed like nothing,
just a pain in the back.
We thought it would pass,
like every scrape, every stubborn moment.

Then, the morning after, the knock at my door —
the priest telling me you were gone,
a bleeding ulcer, they said.
You never told me it hurt that much.

Is it me who keeps you here,
or love that never fades?
Maybe it's the weight
of my own reflection,
wondering if I've held on too tightly.

Even now, I feel you both,
threaded through the quiet spaces,
just as you were.

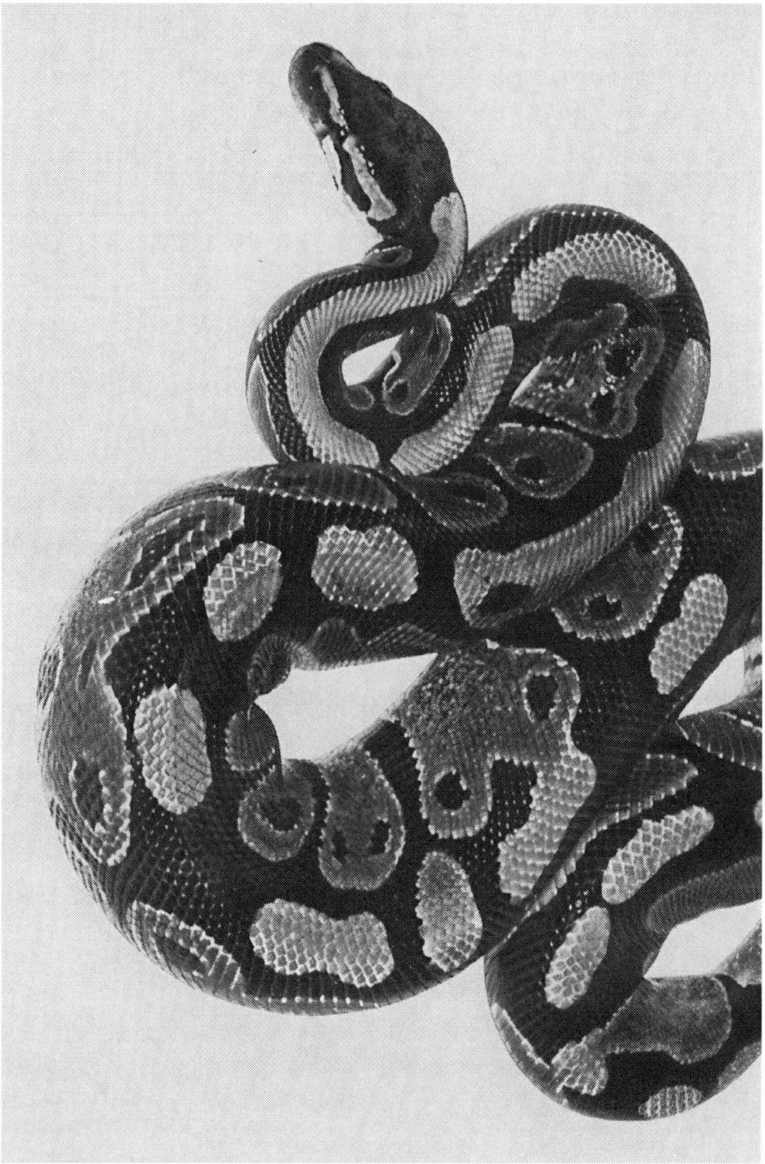

Hideaway

Softly emerging from dusk,
sweet messenger of dawn,
a golden cherub cradled
in a glass globe,
swirling colours —
shimmering hues of red, green, and blue.

Whose heart do you hold,
ever secure in your chubby embrace,
snug within that ethereal sphere?

Seated in the alcove
of this old house,
unburdened by faith,
yet bearing the weight
of a life unlived —
stilled by the coiled python
in my womb.

In the darkness of loss,
I search for a sign,
longing for your angelic touch
to soothe the deep wound inside.

Divine little messenger,
summon sacred songs
from the empyrean.

With your wings, shelter me
from bitter thoughts
that cloud my mind.
In you, I find a spark of consolation —
though disbelief holds my tongue,
you stir my soul.

But I cannot bring back
the precious life
that slipped away.

In this moment, at the edge of day,
your presence offers a brief reprieve —
an illusion I cling to,
if only for an instant.

Cherished angel,
a reminder of love and the burden of love.
In the quiet hours before dawn,
our spirits seem to connect.

Then, abruptly,
I lash out in anger:

To think I am confiding
in such a ridiculous figure —
puny wings of plaster,
blowing a minuscule trumpet,
basking in the feigned celestial glow
of your absurd orb.

In a sudden burst of wrath,
I seize the globe
and let it fall
to the hard tile floor —
angel and all.
Shattering into fragments that mimic
my own disintegration.

I rise from the table
barefoot on watery shards
of broken glass.
Blood and glimmer mix,
a sharp sting underfoot.
I welcome the distraction.

Crawling into bed, I weep —
a familiar exercise
in futility,
wishing for a true hideaway,
a sphere of solace,
for a mother who feels
she has failed.

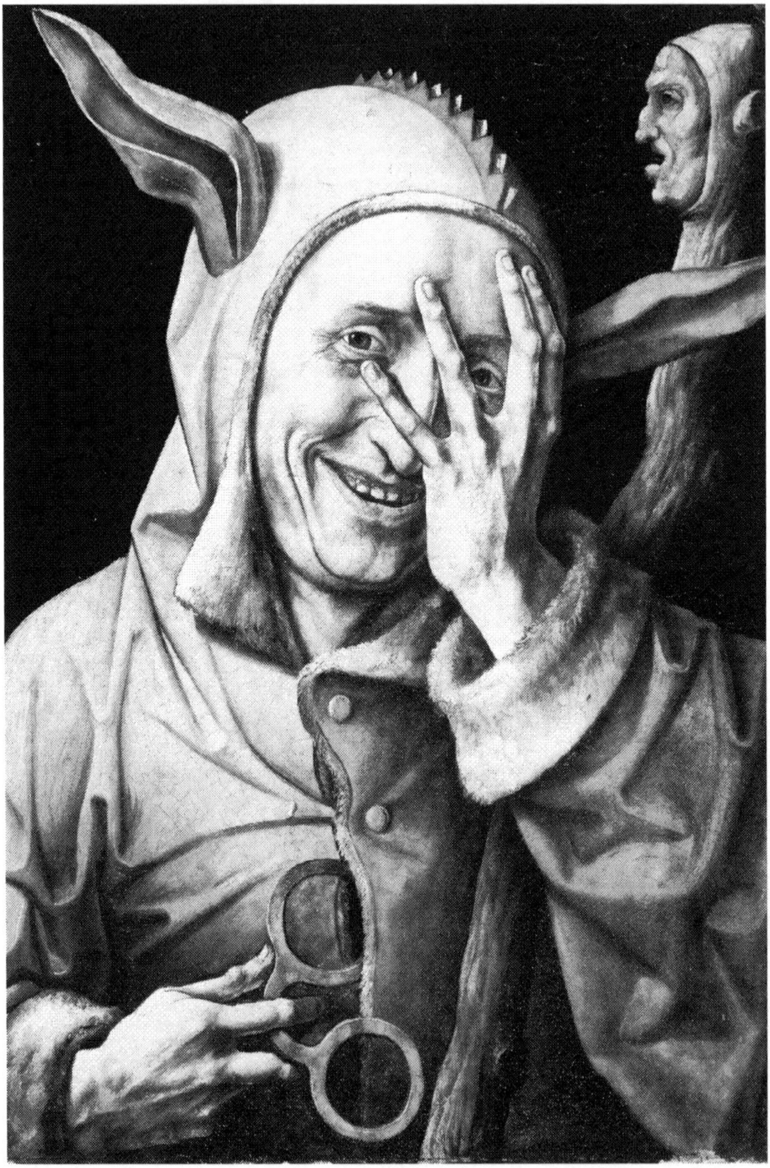

Hidden Fury

In laughter's cloak, I hide my seething rage,
a jester's grin masking the inner fire.
Words, sharp as blades, dance lightly on the stage,
veiled barbs, wrapped in foolery's attire.

Beneath the chuckles, a tempest brews unseen,
each laugh a thunderclap, a silent scream.
Mirthless smiles, a façade so pristine,
hiding truths too raw to redeem.

In this charade of merriment and jest,
lies a silent admission of defeat.
Why bare a soul, when none will invest
in turmoil's depths, bitter and replete?

Laughing away the futility of rage,
for no cry or fury can rewrite the page.
A guise — a balm, or perhaps a cage,
enclosing despair too vast to gauge.

So I don my mask, and with laughter engage,
yet in each quip, a hidden plea — a silent age.
Behind this screen, I quietly wage
a war with shadows on an unseen stage.

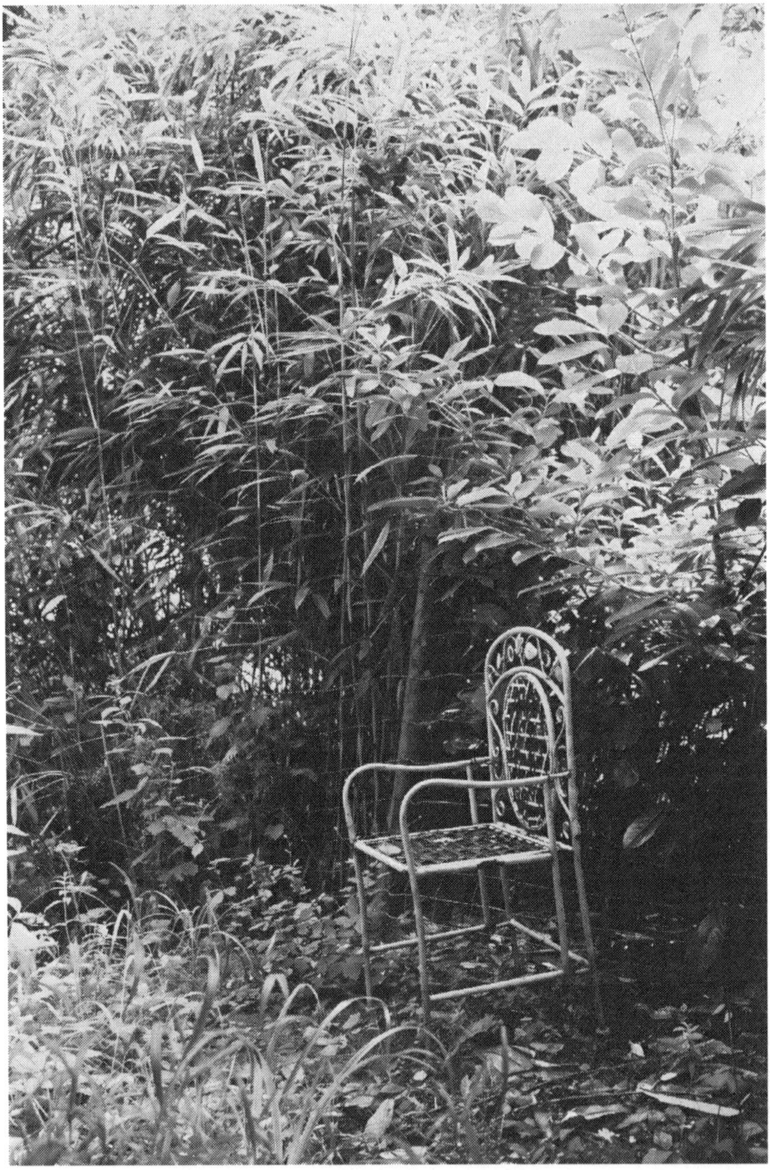

New Neighbours

The empty chair waits a little too long,
anticipating the morning's beauty,
while shadows lengthen and retreat.

 Long underwear hung out to dry;
 spring winds invite them to dance,
 like it or not.

On the eve of Walpurgis Night,
new dimensions open up in space —
stretched light-years ripple to the north.

White caps stuffed with drunken youths
rolling wildly in the grass.
Their laughter spins off-balance.

Tiimo, godfather to the harmonica,
Fiigo, and the household dog —
none of them speak Swedish.

Bodies gather in the corner,
a most alarming find during house search;
such is life.

Children cry in their sleep,
beneath a tattered flag,
from an old spin dryer.

Sorrow and nostalgia,
new neighbours,
peer deeply into our eyes.

The magical moment arrives,
unheralded, quiet,
and time moves on.

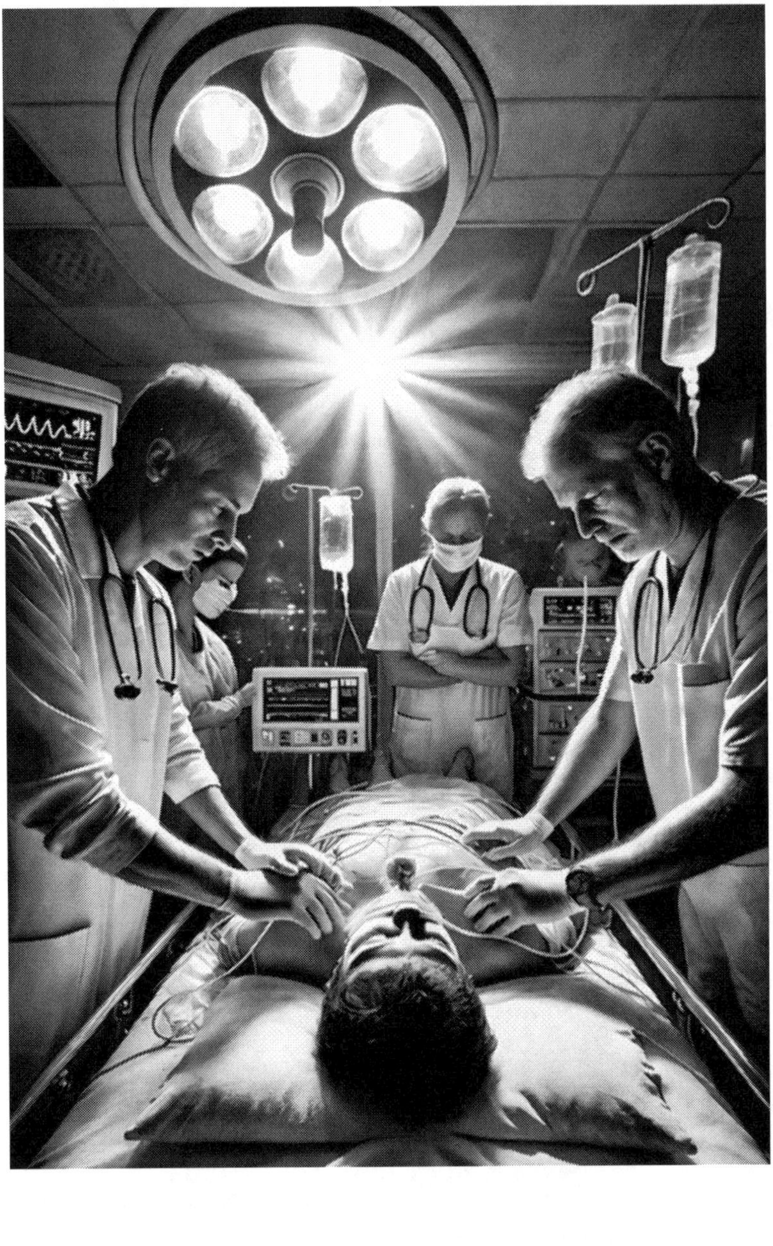

The Race Against Silence
Patient: James Oliver Smith

"Doctor quick, doctor quick,"
urgent, resounding through the halls,
a summons to action at the pulse of the hospital.

Faint in the distance,
a siren whistles its foreboding song.

We assemble rapidly, movements precise,
our resuscitation crew united
in a tug of war with time,
monitors beep a constant cadence,
reflecting the swiftness in our steps.

Hands press rhythmically —
vitality pitted against stillness,
each compression a resolute effort
to awaken a heartbeat.

The din of a dauntless fight with the odds.

Amid the chaos, unnoticed,
water trickles, drip, drip, from a faucet on the wall.

Air hisses through the ventilation tube,
mechanical gasps,
in harmony with our steadfast actions,
our focus as sharp as the stakes are high.

"Ready, and clear." Energy surges,
adrenaline courses directly,
a final entreaty to the torpid core,
fluttering on the brink,
hesitating, then steadying,
a rhythm reborn, triumph in every throb.

Outside, an agony of suspense.
The waiting room gathers a tapestry of faces.

A young girl's whispered question to her father
threading softly through the tense tableau.

A teenagers booted foot taps anxiously,
siblings' glances repeatedly drawn
toward the portal to unknown outcomes,
looks dart, fingers twist,
every silent pause an unspoken plea.

The double door swings open, the team leader enters,
a meeting of gazes, silence pregnant,
the gnawing ache of shared awaiting
discernible in the quiet.

"Stable," he says, the word like a salve.
Eyes widen, a flow of ease begins to spread,
a collective sigh, solace and gratitude mingling,
worried expressions give way to thankful smiles,
here, where the thread of existence holds strong.
Light of calm washes over, dispelling unrest,
subdued joy, bear hugs exchanged in solidarity.

Beyond, the siren's blare now at the hospital's door.

Then, rising above it all,
"Doctor quick! doctor quick! doctor quick!"
Through these passages,
each alert flags a precarious margin,
at the cusp of moments birthing and fading,
the perpetual interplay
between hope and departure unfolds.

In this realm, where time bends
to the rhythm of heartbeats,
eternity lingers in every breath.

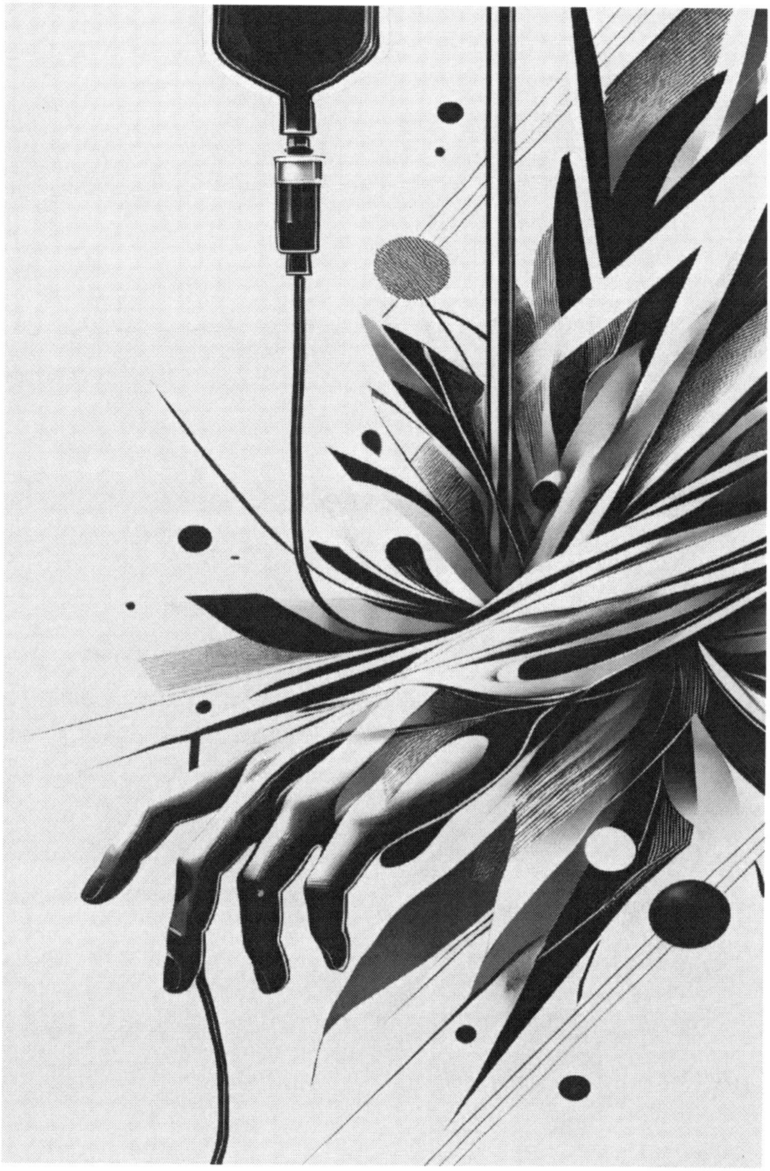

The Unyielding Hour
Patient: James Oliver Smith

A shout from loudspeakers pierces the bustle
within these walls alive with activity.
"Doctor quick! doctor quick!"

A clock ticks relentlessly, marking unseen seconds.

We gather from all directions,
our response swift, objective distinct,
meticulous orchestration under the taut flatline.

A highly focused confrontation by the final exit.

Chest compressions, relentless and rigorous,
despite the troubling sound of breaking ribs,
still hoping for a sign.

Growing closer, the siren's wail cuts through the air.

Each push a battle
against eternal repose,
vital support methodically sustained,
drugs flood the veins, a fervent chemical appeal.

"Shock now." A pause, a blink, anticipation,
but the trace remains flat, an implacable refusal.
"More adrenaline." Injected straight to the heart,
yet the signal persists, unwavering.
Finally, the reluctant pronouncement.
"Call it."

In the waiting room, trust mingles with fear,
apprehension with tension.

The young mother clutching her child,
an elderly man's furrowed brow.

Nearby, a solitary figure paces, restless,
tracing paths of optimism and worry —
while a couple stands in a tight embrace.
Silent stares fixate on the entrance,
a gateway to fates unknown.

Anxiety's cloak draped over the room,
dark and stifling.
Murmurs of comfort,
fragile words amidst uncertainties,
a sense of dread seeps into the atmosphere,
heartbeats counting questions unanswered.

The door opens, the leader emerges,
heads turn, a hush falls.
"We did everything we could," a gentle, heavy truth.
A wave of grief, the reality of loss setting in.

Here, where life and death's fine line
is quietly crossed, their sorrow,
laden with unvoiced farewells,
casts its shadow dimly through the corridors.

Outside, the siren's blare now at the hospital's door.

Then, rising above it all,
"Doctor quick! doctor quick! doctor quick!"
Through these passages,
each alert flags a precarious margin —
at the cusp of moments birthing and fading,
the perpetual interplay
between hope and departure unfolds.

In this realm, where time ceases
with the fall of silence,
a single instant bears the weight of forever.

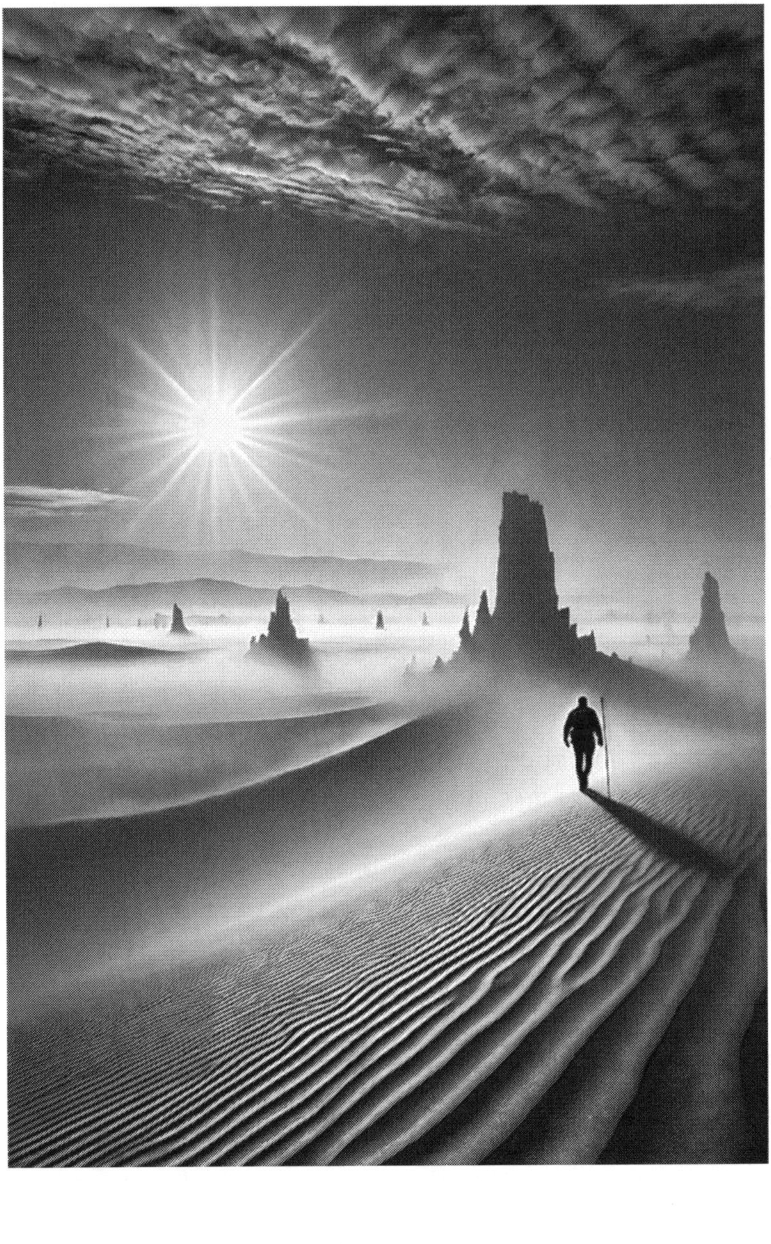

Bedrock of Change

Extending into the near distance,
plains unending, submerged in mist,
a vast absence of lasting purpose,
drifting in time, the soul surrenders.

Blinded by doubt and dark despair,
a lone traveller staggers onward,
pursuing paths to escape from illusion,
leading perpetually to looming mirages.

An endless trek under a fierce sun,
following trails of bloodstained spoors,
lost in halls of myths and mirrors,
trapped between Beast and Beauty.

Perhaps an oasis of hope lies hidden,
longing for water in a desert of death,
salvaged from thirsty waves of sand
by fresh springs flowing from the earth.

A fertile island in an ocean of drought,
founded upon a bedrock of change,
settled by those in search of life
who dare to embrace the winds of thought.

Launch, beloved creature, from the shore,
touch the song of a bird in flight,
kiss the tears shed by children of trees,
listen to colours hiding quietly in the shade.

Ride a high storm
through turbulent times,
recall the future,
the road we must find,
lest circling vultures mistake us for dead,
courage and conscience guiding our tread.

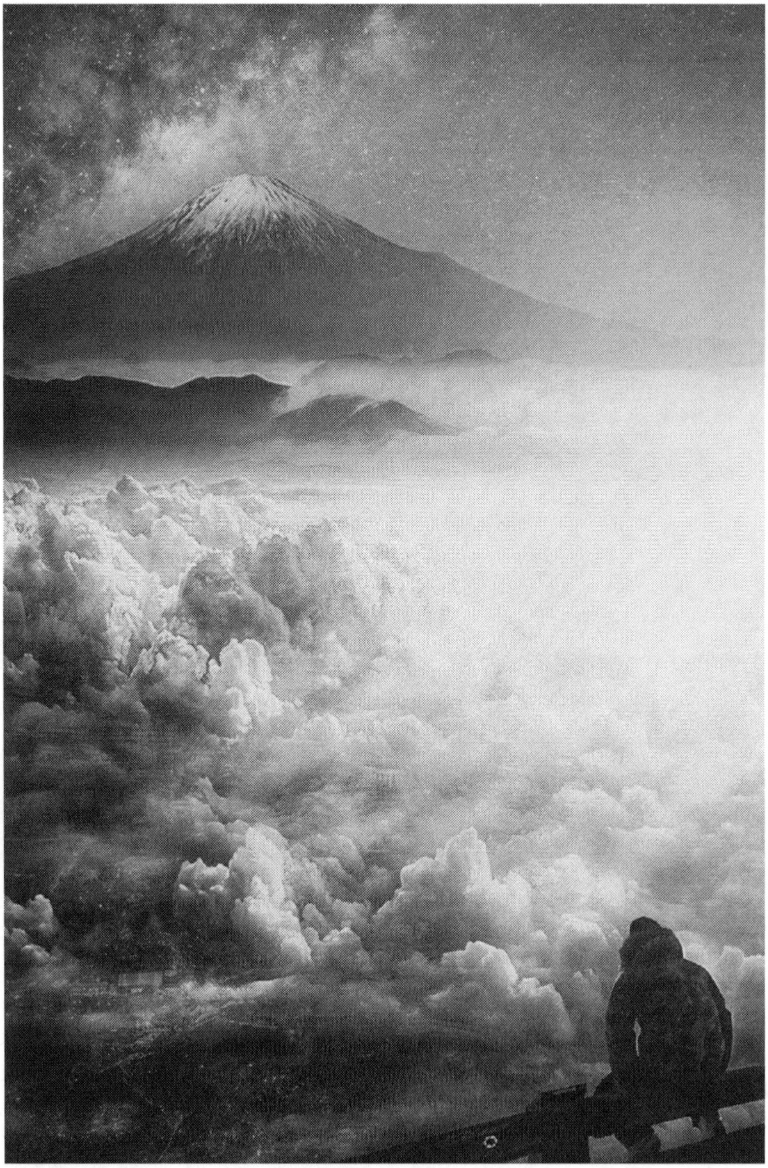

Poetry in Motion

He was born to northern winds,
a child who grew within the storm.
As seasons shifted, standing tall —
his body etched with trails of travel.

From windswept cliffs beneath his feet,
to rivers cut through timeless rock,
bringing men into the wild,
where earth and sky collide.

Shaped by trials that tested him,
shadows circling near and far,
will tempered, heart held firm.
His story lives in ink on flesh,
"Invictus" an unwavering compass —
written on his skin.

"Out of the night that covers me,
Black as the pit from pole to pole,
I thank whatever gods may be
For my unconquerable soul."

The gales that once howled and raged
now carry his quiet strength
to every corner of the land
he calls home.
Visitors follow, unaware
of burdens borne,
battles faced,
and blows weathered.

"In the fell clutch of circumstance
I have not winced nor cried aloud.
Under the bludgeonings of chance
My head is bloody, but unbowed."

With every turn of the wheel,
as he leads them across glacial plains,
they feel the calm in steady hands —
hands that have braved far more
than the biting breath of the Arctic.

"Beyond this place of wrath and tears
Looms but the Horror of the shade,
And yet the menace of the years
Finds, and shall find, me unafraid."

In the silent beauty of the wilderness,
where summits watch the world below,
he is poetry in motion —
his journey carved into the earth,
as ancient forces of nature
have left their trace upon him.

"It matters not how strait the gate,
How charged with punishments the scroll,
I am the master of my fate:
I am the captain of my soul."

And so he stands, resolute,
on the threshold of his domain.
The mountains, the rivers, the endless sky —
reflected in his gaze,
as he belongs to them, and they to him.

"Invictus" by William Ernest Henley.

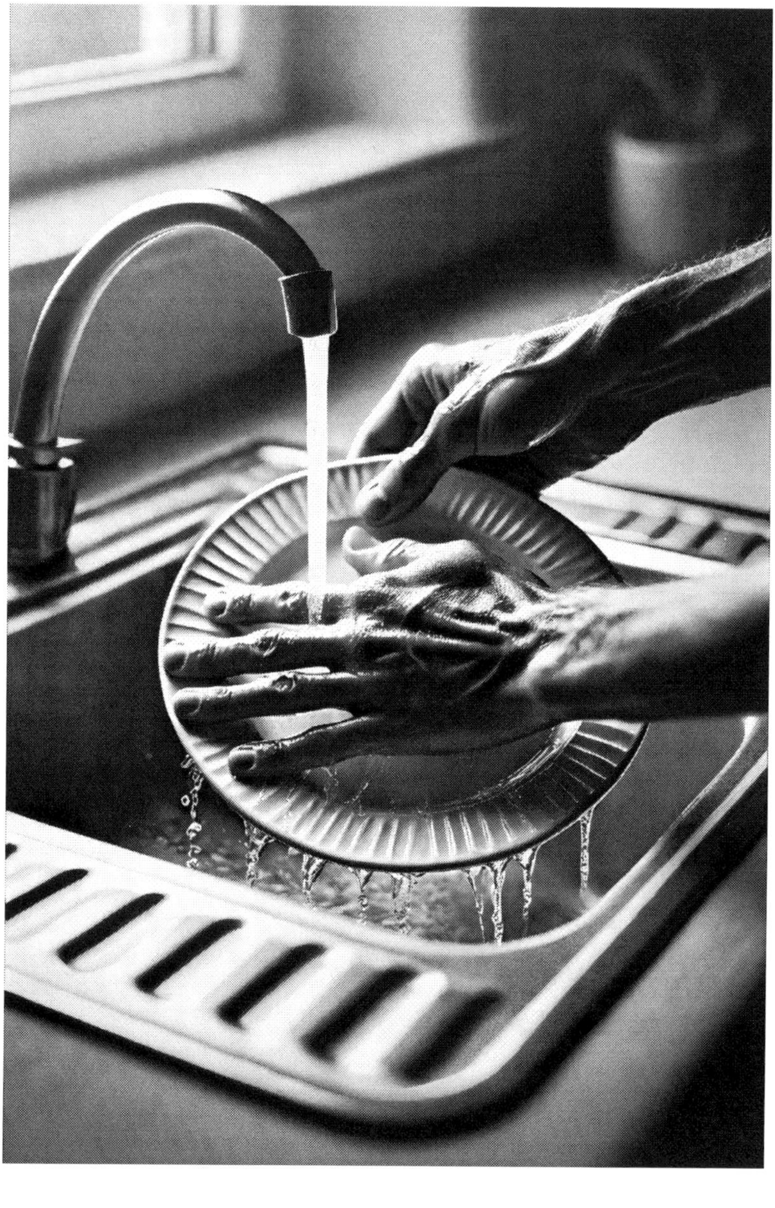

Burgers and Fries

We always dine accompanied by
the evening news.

Lovingly I say:
"Please, pass me that platter of human agony."

You hand it over, your face a mask of indifference:
"Think I'd like some shrill cries
of people clinging to the last shred of hope."

Strangers visit our home every night —
ghostly figures
on the television screen.
We watch them with unease come and go,
hoping they won't outstay their welcome.

The sizzle of beef, the scent of frying potatoes,
ketchup's tang on my tongue.

A desperate woman runs to and fro
in a street far from ours,
her face distorted with fear,
delivering her line against the sound of bombs:

What am I supposed to do with my children?

You glance up, looking bored,
declare, "I've got this,"
as we finish eating.
"Thank you," I say,
"but remember to wash off the blood."

I turn off the TV,
there's nothing new anyway,
just another rerun,
same tragedy, different day.

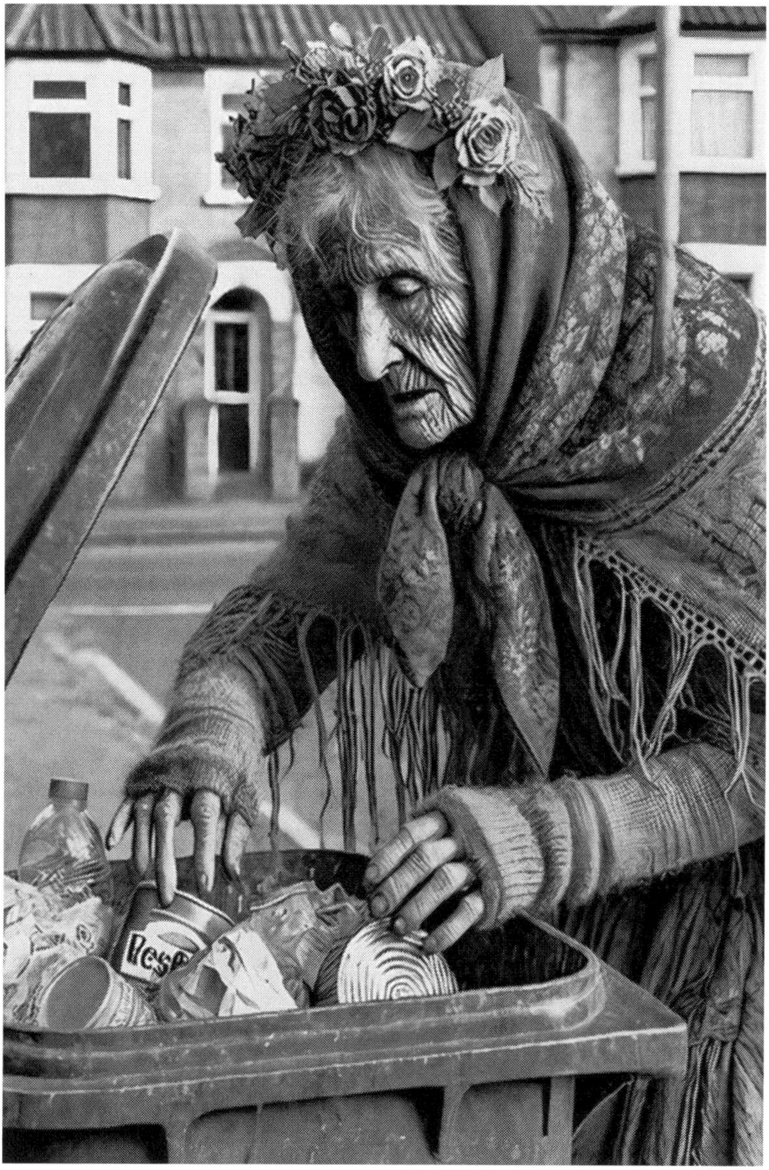

Misericorde

There — that sound again!
Tomorrow is pickup day
and the crone returns to her old beat.
Gnarled hands rummage
in my rubbish, her livelihood.

Flowers on her tattered scarf
whip in the careless wind.
Her face — a cracked shell
guarding humiliation.

I peer out the window,
watching her sift through my waste.
Why does she do this
for all to witness —
expose my secrets, her misery,
to the scrutiny of daylight?

She looks up and sees me,
my arch compassion:
There but for the grace of God go I.

Laughter roars in her eyes.
She meets my gaze:
The grace of God, is it?
She knows —
I think we are worlds apart.

Her grin twists
around the thought:
Home is where the heart is...
But yours? It's grown cold, hasn't it?

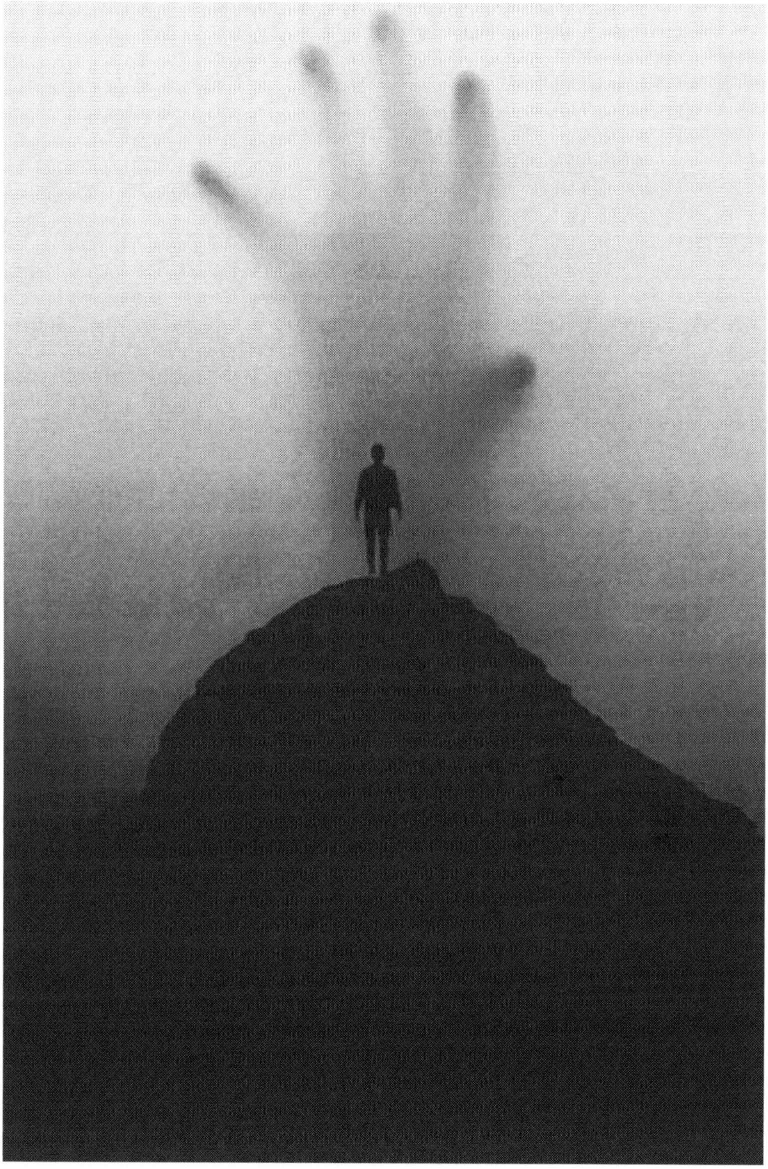

Veil of Kindness

Cruel in his compassion,
the benevolent man
coats harsh reality,
inflicting subtle pain.

White lies are worms,
feasting on deceit,
malignant crawlies
gnawing at the core of trust.

The host who harbours them —
hidden behind an elegant mask
of pretense and illusion,
confined within walls of need,
yearning for the balm of validation.

Ignoring the truth it cannot bear,
the fractured self craves nothing more
than the comfort of insidious falsehoods.

Bound to their presence,
it seeks refuge, greedily guzzling
the seductive venom
of hollow solace and complacency.

Entrapped in this cycle,
clarity fades,
a faint echo in a chamber of delusion,
while the veil of kindness
conceals the festering wounds beneath.

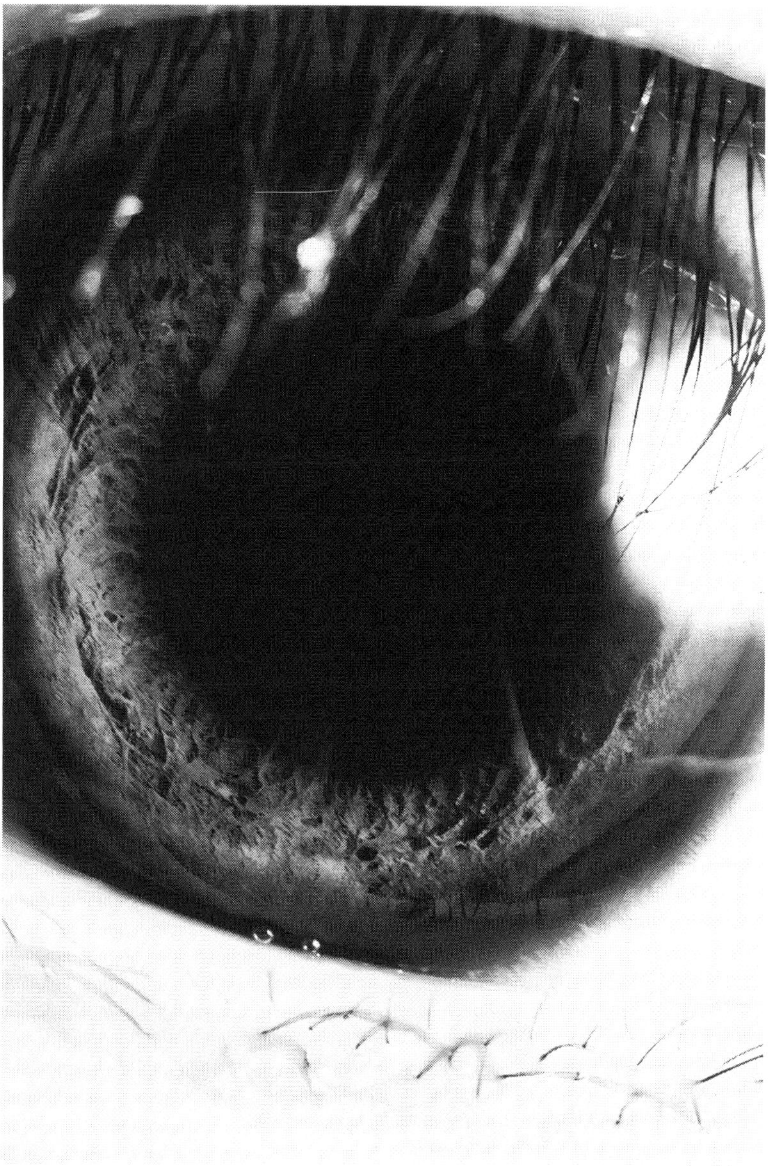

Violations

"If thine eye offend thee, pluck it out!"
Pluck it out?
Yes, as simple as that.
Fumble gently, then a swift tug,
like ripping off a plaster.

Dribble the eyeball lightly with your fingertips,
then grasp it firmly
and cast it from thee,
send it soaring into the sky.

Watch with your solitary gaze,
unblinking, as it arcs above,
tracing the curve of existence.
Caught in the sun's glare,
it whips around, continuing its journey.

Ensnared in its own orbit, sight perceives
everything it believes
there is to see.
What does it discern?
Is it God in His heaven?
Manifestations of the Universal Mind?
Or perhaps silent space, without meaning,
an inky abyss, a cosmic chill?

Does vision see only the self —
an eye for an "I",
sloshing in a sea
of isolated souls, unyielding?
Adrift, alone, floating in the void,
where no one can hear them scream.

In the beginning, vision strayed.
Temptation paused, waiting.
The first eye gone, a trade of sight for purity.

But alas, desire calls again.
For absolute purity,
remove your other eye.

Then sever an arm,
for it, too, has led you astray.
One? No, both. Let's not hesitate.
Slice them in one swift motion,
a quick cut, a clean break.

Next, no small feat
for one so diminished:
cast the whole lot
into a cauldron gargantuan,
a world sightless, but free from sin.

Arms juggling eyes,
the stories they've seen,
creation in all its hues, shades, and sensations.
Inside the metagalactic kitchen,
the monstrous cauldron is heating up fast.

Plucked eyes simmer on top,
crushed to pulp
by the sinewy embrace
of sundry arms,
stewing in their own juices.

"For verily, verily, I say unto thee:"
anything is better than falling
into temptation.

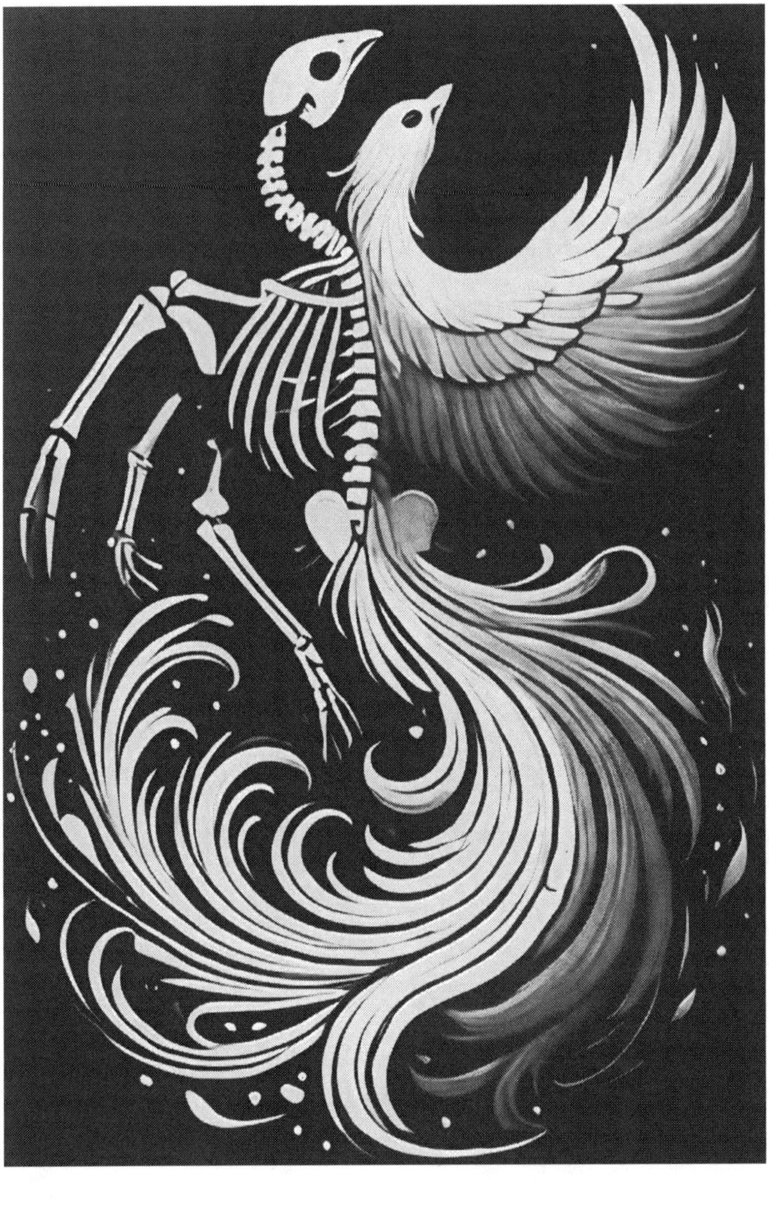

Alicorn

Bleeding, the weary sun and I
rise warily from the firebird's ashes.
Another dawn, stillborn,
child of apathy and despair,
of runaway fury and ferocity.

Clouds, like leeches, cling to dying light;
scarlet rain seeps into parched earth.

A fireball plummets toward the depths,
that wingless torch
of sleeping flesh and bone,
a tale of myth and sorrow
left unsung.

Thunder nearby heralds doom,
foretold by the creature's torn and tortured cry.
Pale riders gather,
closing in at ground zero.

Raptors, grotesque, circle the poisoned lake,
round and round forever, razor beaks
smirking at their own reflections.

Cowering tomorrows writhe
in the unyielding grip of hooked talons —
an insatiable cavern hides unspoken grief.

Starkly, I see through myself now,
a core of embers, a heart of cold stone.
If it breaks, the sculptor's not to blame;
eir chisel seeks a finer form.

The unicorn, elusive, means no harm
to those who impale themselves
on the spiralling horn.

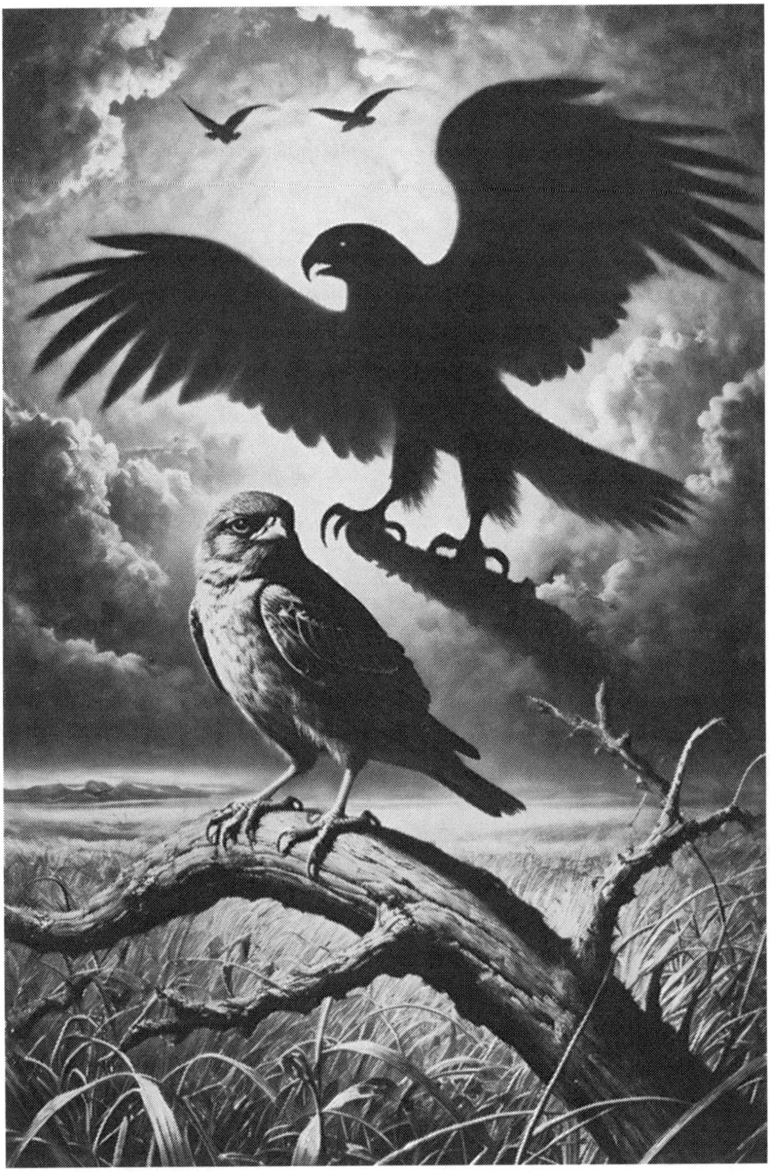

Strength From Struggle:
A Journey of Growth
Across the Shifting Sands of Our Times

In the blur of early years,
where time and place softly blend,
at age three, my world was a small haven,
cradled in loving parental arms —
boundless, yet safe.

Next door lived a boy, my partner in play,
together we explored the garden outside home.

We created worlds on our golden stage,
a land vibrant under joint command,
whims the law in this imaginary space.

With minds wide open, stories spun,
the sandbox our grand kingdom —
monarchs of a crafted realm,
in fantasy we won
crowns of sand, sceptres of creation.

Masters of make-believe,
gods of brainstorms —
we declared ourselves rulers,
reigning over sand and pebbles.

One day, as the sun shone in our eyes,
an airplane's silhouette sparked a chase.

"Let's race it!" I shouted,
without a second thought.
Our laughter rang out,
breaths quickening,
as we ran wildly,
small legs at flying pace,
reaching beyond the treetops.

Fields unfolded
into pathways of flight.
Spellbound, I gazed upward,
locking eyes with a distant pilot.

In that moment, the ground tilted,
positions crossed —
as I rose, the pilot's view became mine.

The wind lifted me, higher and higher —
a city stretched beneath,
alive with movement.
Earth swept toward the horizon,
a spectrum of colours,
until the sea appeared.

Emerald isles dotted the blue expanse,
charged with the thrill of discovery,
a dance of varied clues.
Gripped by a sense of danger, I hovered,
caught between exhilaration and fear.

I grew wings that year.
Soaring, free,
no longer tethered to the earth.

But then, a gentle touch, a soothing voice
called me back from such unknown heights
to the safety of home.
The real world, clear yet changed —
the lines between reality and fantasy thinned.

Bridging worlds, the boy, the pilot, and I,
connected across shifting sands of time.
We found truth in dreams
under the vast sky.

Whitherward Bound 1938 — A Passage into Deeper Currents

Our home, alive with joyful play in the sunny garden,
touched by the warmth of love,
and a taste for adventure,
now resounded with the snap of closing suitcases —
signals of our farewell,
as we left behind the life
created in Copenhagen's safe fold.

"What about the sandbox?" I asked, my voice trembling,
the earthy smell still lingering in my nostrils.

"It stays here," Dad replied, calm and reassuring,
gently patting my head. With a smile
that crinkled the corners of his eyes, he added,
"But you can bring your kingdom."

A journey was imminent —
by train and ferry, then train again —
reaching from Denmark's shores
to Heidelberg's portal into a future.

The city held secrets and deep mysteries,
beyond childhood's simple sketches,
awaiting our footprints, revealing new realms,
ready to engage all my senses,
awakening me to an array of impressions.

***

At daybreak, the silence was shattered
by the piercing wail of a whistle.

As the platform drifted away,
a startling realization struck me —
it wasn't the earth that moved, but us
propelled in concert
with the measured rumble of the tracks.

This relentless beat, like a broken record,
played on and on in my head,
each turn advancing our journey.

The constant clatter
was a persistent backdrop
to my reflections.

***

The ferry's deck opened before us,
an infinite expanse of sea stretched wide.
Vast like the skies above our old house,
it shared ancient tales with the curious.

Refreshing and raw,
the brisk salty gusts,
laced with the essence of brine,
mingled with the invigorating spray
misting my face.

As the horizon broadened,
memories of my past flight stirred,
rekindling the thrill
of boundless freedom.

Below, jellyfish glided near the water's edge,
their delicate bodies translucent,
enchanting.

Aglow under the sun's soft caress,
graceful forms undulating
in the ocean's currents.

The sight recalled the smoothness
of cold glass under my fingertips.
Their sleek texture imagined
while my mother held me up to see.

"Can I play with them?" I wondered out loud,
captivated by the fluid grace of their dance.

"Mind the sting," she cautioned,
her grip tightening protectively over my hand,
a firm reminder of the hidden perils
beneath the sea's inviting surface.

"But they're beautiful," I said,
my stare fixed in fascination.
"Sometimes, beauty can be deceiving,"
she answered gently.

***

Mighty wheels sang a low,
mournful song against the rails,
echoing through the faintly lit carriage.
Hints of coal and smoke, with an acrid bite
that coated my tongue, floated in
as we traversed beneath the starry sky.

Sharp against the tranquil fragrance of fresh linen,
infusing the crisp sheets that enveloped us
within our dim berth.

Through the dead of night,
confined within the cabin's narrow spaces,
I tasted the bitter tang of oiled steel.
The haunting melody of chains in passage
sounded in the darkness,
linking each car with a ghostly keening.

"Trains are like horses, they talk in their sleep,"
my father's voice emerged through the gloom, playful.
Drowsy but intrigued, I asked, "What do they say?"
"They describe dreams of distant trails
they've yet to explore," he responded
in his resonant baritone.

The quiet concern of my parents,
a steady undercurrent,
rippled through the stillness, subtly pervasive,
sinking into the depths of my young heart.
Their hushed words hung heavy,
like evening primrose's perfume
in the cool breeze,
filling private recesses with unspoken love.

Whispers, like the gentle rustling of leaves,
or the graze of feathers against my consciousness,
wove through the atmosphere,
evoking a swirling murmuration of starlings at sunrise,
a ballet of shadows in twilight.

***

Day chased away the dark.
Our iron horse edged forward,
Dad vanished into the crowd to fetch a newspaper.
"Will he find his way back?" I said, barely audible.
Mom squeezed my hand, "He always does."

The buttery aroma of almond croissants,
sweet and mouthwatering,
drifted from the nearby vendor
and blended with the morning's first sigh,
arousing a longing for the
comforting breakfasts we used to have,
tugging at my awareness,
a brief distraction from the mounting anxiety.

Each second stretched, my chest tightened
with fear of losing him among so many.
I held my breath and watched,
until his welcome shape returned,
hastening back as the locomotive
hummed its readiness —
intense relief washed over me when he stepped aboard.

His clean scent, mixed with a trace of antiseptic,
wrapped around me like a warm blanket,
conjuring memories of my favourite bedtime stories,
a presence of security in the turbulence of transit.
The engine's soothing rumble
marked our route onward.

***

This first brush with fear,
and the sting of tears,
permanently etched in a child's memory,
began to unravel a new understanding —
that our surroundings
were more than just havens of play.
Beyond the familiar,
the world was fraught with challenges,
tales of peace disrupted, as lives transformed.

So, I grasped the unsteady tide of existence,
rising slowly at times,
serenely lulling,
then crashing with startling speed and relentless force.

Our path, a kaleidoscope of motion,
led us into territories unknown,
unveiling different dimensions,
shifting "home" from merely a place
to a spectrum of enriching experiences.

Each step resonated with the crunch
of uncharted ground beneath our feet,
a transition from childhood's sanctuary
to a panorama rich with joy, sorrow,
and profound insights.

"Does it ever end?" I mused aloud.
"Only when we stop searching for novel perspectives,"
came the thoughtful reply.

The air around us, tinged with a whiff of pine,
enlivened our spirits,
each scene a precise stitch, crafting our quilt
across dynamic landscapes.
Winds, heavy with remnants of historic stone,
swept through us,
as the enduring rhythm of dusk and dawn
coloured the golden hours.

The City of Contrasts — Songs and Shadows

Heidelberg unfolds like an ancient manuscript,
recounting tales of poets and philosophers,
resting delicately along the line that divides
past reflections from the present's gaze,
where history teeters between
the tangible and the enigmatic.

The heavens gather,
sensing an impending storm,
the atmosphere thick with the threat
of rain and thunder.

Our new home hides behind an ivied façade —
where the legacy of centuries
meets daily rhythm.
Mom unpacks, her words soothing
amidst the changes,
while Dad, a surgeon, works tirelessly at the hospital.

The smell of fresh bread from nearby bakeries
intertwines with the mustiness of aged stone.
From our window,
the castle rises steadfast,
often destroyed yet always rebuilt,
its red sandstone walls in harmony
with the green hills
and the winding Neckar River below.

Cobblestone lanes, narrow and bending,
lead to the Old Bridge, where the Neckar's earthy scent
greets the refreshing fragrance
of surrounding forests,
stirring the senses in the soft glow of dawn.

Church bells chime,
their notes blending with the tram's clang,
and the melodies of wandering musicians
resound through the square.

In the bustling marketplace, a towering man,
black-clad and boisterous, addresses a gathering,
his strident rhetoric burying ordinary concerns.
Pedestrians quicken their pace, driven by unease,
their conversations a mix of market haggling
and hushed voices.

Stalls laden with fruits, cheeses, and meats
entice with the savoury hint of sausages grilling,
street food sizzling in vendor carts.

Spires soar towards the firmament
above the bastion of learning,
entangled with doctrines of a sinister era.
The university, once a centre of fearless debate,
carefully balances on the tightrope of censorship,
cautious murmurs of diligent scholars
mingling with the aura of timeworn books and ink.

Overrun by swarms of SA and SS members,
their beloved city now a stronghold
of Nazism's repressive influence.

Between historic buildings,
stretched clotheslines
form a vibrant cat's cradle of the mundane.
Trolleys glide along their tracks,
mechanisms I understand.

Garments flutter,
displaying the persistence of routines,
in a community bracing for the unknown.

Through the layers of what is
and what might be,
I wander the alleys,
a tiny god of lost things,
my laughter a misplaced key
in the pocket of approaching war.

The kindergarten, which looks cheerful on the outside,
conceals ominous messages
beneath its veneer —
"Vorwärts! Vorwärts! Schmettern die hellen Fanfaren"
we sing with innocent abandon,
"Forwards! Forwards!
Blare the bright fanfares" —
unaware of the grave implications behind the verse.

One morning, Mom thinks I might be ill,
placing a thermometer to check.
Worried I won't be singing with my friends,
I wiggle, causing it to slip.
Glass breaks, mercury scatters
like lost moons across the floor.

Curious, I reach out,
trying to gather quicksilver beads.
But just then, as the silvery droplets elude my grasp,
I begin to perceive the fading of carefree days.

***

Awakened by voices and anguished crying,
I creep towards the kitchen,
cloaked in darkness.
Usually warm with the sweet aromas of Mom's cooking,
the room now brims with a sorrow I can't understand.

Hugo, Dad's colleague and family friend,
weeps uncontrollably, his feelings intertwining
with theirs in shared despair.
Slumped in his brown SA uniform,
a reluctant participant in the horror of events,
haunted by the spectre of Kristallnacht,
when the absence of light took form.

The Night of Broken Glass,
illuminated by the shards of falling stars,
when shattered windows and torn lives
marred the soul of an entire nation,
fuelled by the rising tide
of hate and propaganda.

He describes the violence he witnessed and enacted —
shops destroyed, synagogues burned,
and countless futures forever stifled.

His eyes that normally overflow with laughter,
are dulled by sadness and regret,
the terror of those hours etched deeply into his being.

My parents' tears flow for the tragedy
that befell so many, for the twisting pain and guilt
of their compassionate friend,
a marionette strung by fate,
torn between obedience and defiance.

Mom's gentle nudging leads me back to bed,
but the weight of grief and the tension around us
introduces me to a world much larger
and more frightening than I have known before.

Later I ask, "Why didn't he just say No?"
"Sometimes No is a really big word," they respond.
"One that demands tremendous courage."

***

Winter thaws into spring.
Carnival's energy,
alive with song and dance,
stands in sharp opposition
to the perilous undertow.

We call it Fasching,
when everyone is jolly and foolish.
Enormous striding figures captivate my young eyes,
painted puppets animated by hidden performers
enhance the excitement.

With my parents and Hugo by my side,
deep tones of large horns resonate,
trumpets blare in jubilant symphony,
flooding the surroundings with festive fanfares.
The crisp breeze carries promises
of candy floss and taffy apples.

Yet beneath the laughter,
a shadow lingers, a tension unspoken,
as if the world is frozen in its tracks.

Lifting me onto his shoulders,
perhaps seeking redemption in the eyes of a child,
Hugo makes me feel part of the spectacle,
rising above the crowd.

We move through the lively thoroughfares,
embraced by the cheerful chaos all around,
though I notice his grip tighten,
a silent reminder of what he hopes to forget.

Dazzling costumes spin wildly,
like tops gone mad.
"Look at their outfits!" I shout,
pointing to the colourful characters,
their joyful dance
a counterpoint to the cool air.

For my fourth birthday,
he gave me a shiny musical toy,
a gift that now feels like an invitation
to partake in the fun.

"Go on, play along," he urges, and I do,
my unbridled glee one with the pulse of the parade,
as if my innocent music could drown out
the echoes of a world teetering on the brink.

We enter a busy restaurant,
alive with the spirit of the carnival.
An orchestra appears on stage,
setting an enchanting mood.
Boldly I step onto the platform,
toy saxophone at the ready,
releasing simple, unrefined sounds,
performing in the show with great confidence.

For a moment, the weight of the world melts away.
The spectres of worry retreat,
replaced by pure, unfiltered joy.

The patrons smile and clap,
their faces beaming with delight.
The creativity of a child's imagination
offers a brief escape
from the complexities of our world.

My earnest tune of celebration
brightens the greyness of dread,
colours of pure joy and the wonder of childhood,
a solace for those caught in the pulsing wait of time.

Even as the music fades,
the shadows return, hovering at the edges,
a reminder that the carnival is but a fleeting respite.

***

After Fasching, the rainy morning feels dreary,
mom is sobbing in her favourite chair.
I place my teddy in her lap for comfort.
Dad hasn't come home, and she is afraid.

He's been making waves at the Frauenklinik,
protesting forced abortions and sterilizations
of those the regime deems "unworthy of life."
She is terrified the SS has picked him up.

As it turns out, he was out drinking
with his buddy Dimitrov,
communist leader and anti-Nazi.

This is the second time fear's icy fingers
clutch at my heart,
the first time
I am angry with Father.

When I next draw a family picture,
I make him the smallest one —
maybe I was too young to understand.

Once the rain stops,
the sky clears to a radiant blue.
Walking with Mom
up a sloping path towards the castle,
we see a procession of boys in military-style attire,
banners with strange symbols whipping in the wind.

Black lopsided crosses stand out
against the bold fabric.

I break free, compelled to join their march,
eager to chase the mysterious emblems.
"Oddur, come back!"
her call cuts through the commotion.

***

Going with her into the grand concert hall,
a place amazing yet intimidating,
she leads me to a room full of children,
then disappears into a sea of dark figures,
leaving me adrift in currents of music,
both solemn and strange.

Feeling engulfed, I flee,
finding her among many,
seated in a vast, murky hall.
Under an eerie green spotlight,
a formidable black piano stands looming.
The pianist plays Beethoven's "Moonlight Sonata,"
its wistful melody fills the room
with a haunting presence,
still lingering in my memory.

Back then, Luna hid her face
behind a dense cloud,
deaf to the din of the netherworld.
I cry out for Mom. "Mamma! Mamma!"
The anxiety of being lost overpowers my awe.
Seeing my distress, she swiftly comforts me,
leading me away to safety.

This is the third time I've felt real fear.
As I look back now, the concert illustrates
the stark contrast of that period:
Rich cultural heritage against brutal aggression.

***

Navigating my youth through Heidelberg's avenues,
where learning intersects with harsh realities,
life imparts lessons in managing growth,
influenced by an age both rich and ominous.

Evening settles, painting the landscape in muted hues,
tracing silhouettes that dance upon the river's surface.

Students gather in dimly lit pubs,
their mirth an antidote
to the sobering truths of the day,
their dreams interwoven
with the enduring spirit of this place,
a mixture of resilience and melancholy.

As night descends,
the city's heartbeat slows,
constellations shimmer, revealing secrets of the past.

In Heidelberg, the weight of history remains,
reminding of cultural heights and
depths of human cruelty,
of humanity's endless quest for meaning
amidst catastrophe.

Copenhagen, April 9th, 1940 — A Day When Light Dimmed

Tomorrow, I will be five years old,
aware now of when and where I am.
Laughter wanes with the sun's farewell.
Our garden, once a playground of light and shadow,
gently fades to dusk.

Now silent,
the sandbox hides our crowns,
remnants of days rich with adventure
murmuring beneath the sand.

In our apartment, the floor is covered
with greenish linoleum,
where my tin tank sits quietly —
rubber tracks idle.
Whenever I push it, sparks burst from its barrel,
child's play mimicking
battles I don't understand.

I marvel at the tank, now,
reflecting on my parents' choice,
peaceful yet bringing war toys
under our roof.
For my fifth birthday,
a "Wave Warrior" speedboat joins the fleet,
its tiny gun powered by petroleum jelly,
a toy echoing real artillery
of distant battlefields.

Just the day before,
planes crossed the skies.
Later, I learned
they were German warplanes,
bound for Norway.

The next day, tricked by a "friend,"
I lost my new boat.
Small losses foreshadowing greater thefts —
innocence of youth
caught in the crawl of war.
Weapons and conflict seep into my life unbidden,
as Europe nears the precipice,
the Sudetenland just the beginning.

Under the spreading shadow
of a grim dominion,
dawn's early light is overtaken,
the day entirely eclipsed.

As silence deepens,
the city holds its breath.
The King still rides, defiant,
and choosing a path less dark.

Gone without a trace,
the family next door
leaves behind an echoing void,
where joy once filled the air.

My fascination for planes in flight has vanished,
their shapes, once sources of wonder,
now of fear,
casting long shadows
over the lights of my childhood,
warbirds, harbingers of impending danger.

In the quiet, I hear my parents whisper,
a blend of courage and apprehension,
words hang heavy in the air,
carrying the sounds of a world
trembling beneath our feet.

Do you sense it too,
this shift
in the very air we breathe?

Fragments of their dialogue reach me,
talk of occupation, Nazis, Jews,
slowly infiltrating my awareness,
transforming my view
in the relentless winds of change.

Dusk falls,
marking not just today's end,
but the beginning of an undefined era.
We transition from innocence
to profound insight,
shaped by our collective narratives.

Crossing from yesterday into tomorrow,
can we ensure that laughter endures,
sustained by the memory of joy,
even as the lessons of history
slowly unfold?

Will we ever see the full circle —
to realize we are trapped within it?

Bergen in the year 2024 — Echoes of April

Decades leap, my birthday returns.
Underneath April's contemplative sky,
dawn unfurls its quiet light over Bergen.

I embrace the ritual of morning —
oatmeal simmering, blueberries at the brim,
coffee brewing, whispers of steam in the calm.
Everyday gifts of joy,
a simplicity in the safety of my kitchen.

Darkness, my feline companion,
purrs at my feet,
a prelude to the light and shadows
of unfolding hours.

But the day has other plans.
The radio, once a source of morning cheer,
betrays me with news of distant lands aflame,
Gaza's cries piercing through,
a stark intrusion
into my crafted haven of tranquillity.

I reach for the vacuum,
grasping for solace in its steady whirr,
a vain attempt to cleanse my mind.
The hum of machinery only magnifies the chaos,
a poor shield against the world's roar.

The noise cannot mask
the reverberations of a realm in turmoil,
memories and present colliding —
the grim spectre of history repeating,
from the Holocaust's shadows
to Gaza's enduring pain.
Humanity's cycle, a lesson unlearned,
ripples through the safety of my domestic cocoon.

Tears, unbidden, chart their course,
flowing from the boy who once dreamed
beneath endless skies,
to the man, now standing amidst
the remnants of those dreams,
shaped by truths too heavy
to bear alone.

The rain outside
meets my silent reflection,
a subtle rhythm measuring the day's passage.

As watery twilight
blurs the outlines of Bryggen
and boats in the harbour,
a question lingers beneath the ancient sky:

Will we, marked by the wounds
of a shared past,
forge a path
across the shifting sands of our times,
where light dispels the night?

Guided by yesteryear's wisdom,
can we rise toward a dawn
free from sorrow's lasting chains?

Image Sources:

Shear Flow Vortices, cover image
Karl Gaff, own work
Uploaded as part of Wiki Science Competition 2021
Featured picture on Wikimedia Commons
Creative Commons Attribution
4.0 International license
Cropped

Universes of ideas
https://hasanisawi.blogspot.com/2018/11/blog-post.html
Hasanisawi, own work
Creative Commons Attribution-Share Alike 4.0 International license
Cropped, stretched, changed to black and white

Pouring Liquid Gold
Dan Brown, from London, UK
Creative Commons Attribution 2.0 Generic license
Cropped, changed to black and white

Giant ocean wave
Unknown author
Creative Commons CC0
1.0 Universal Public Domain Dedication
Cropped, changed to black and white, shadows

Mirrored half footbridge leading into a snowy forest. Surreal Bridge
Allen McGregor from Brampton, Canada
Creative Commons Attribution 2.0 Generic license.
Cropped, stretched, changed to black and white

Rose
Image generated by OpenAI's DALL-E within DALL-E, facilitated by ChatGPT (GPT-4).
Cropped

Two roses
Image generated by OpenAI's DALL-E within DALL-E, facilitated by ChatGPT (GPT-4).
Cropped

Woman in wheelchair
Image generated by OpenAI's DALL-E within DALL-E, facilitated by ChatGPT (GPT-4).
Cropped

Gauntlet for the Right Hand
Metropolitan Museum of Art
https://www.metmuseum.org/art/collection/search/23255
Creative Commons CC0 1.0
Universal Public Domain Dedication
Cropped, changed to black and white

Sunset on plane, Jacky Lo 2016
Jacky Lo hclojacky
https://unsplash.com/photos/LjX-m_UXQGM
archive copy at the Wayback Machine
Creative Commons CC0 1.0
Universal Public Domain Dedication
Cropped, changed to black and white, enhanced

Realms surpassing reason
Image generated by OpenAI's DALL-E within DALL-E, facilitated by ChatGPT (GPT-4).
Cropped

1968 Warsaw_Pact_invasion_in_Prague_Bild-11638-3.jpg
Vyříznuto z:
https://commons.wikimedia.org/wiki/File:KAS-Prager_Fr%C3%BChling_1968-Bild-11638-3.jpg

Konrad-Adenauer-Stiftung, a German political foundation, as part of a cooperation project.
Archiv für Christlich-Demokratische Politik (ACDP)
Creative Commons Attribution-Share Alike 3.0 Germany license.

Vineyards in Ponte a Bozzone, Tuscany, Italy
https://www.flickr.com/photos/126875359@N03/
Creative Commons Attribution-Share Alike
2.0 Generic license.
Cropped, changed to black and white

Flow and Emotion
Image generated by OpenAI's DALL-E within Book cover designer,
facilitated by ChatGPT (GPT-4).
Cropped

A picture of a mouse in a snowy environment.
https://pixabay.com/photos/snow-mouse-winter-nature-wildlife-3861170/
Alex Kard
Creative Commons CC0 1.0
Universal Public Domain Dedication
Cropped, changed to black and white,

Horse by tree
Image generated by OpenAI's DALL-E within DALL-E,
facilitated by ChatGPT (GPT-4).
Cropped

Still Life with Turtle Hatchling - Turtle Center – Mazunte - Oaxaca – Mexico
Adam Jones from Kelowna, BC, Canada
Creative Commons Attribution-Share Alike 2.0 Generic license.
Cropped, changed to black and white

Person in woods by river
Image generated by OpenAI's DALL-E
through ChatGPT (GPT-4)
Cropped, changed to black and white

My pet ball python - Python royal (Python regius).
Mokele, own work
Creative Commons Attribution-Share Alike 3.0
Unported license.
Cropped, changed to black and white

Portrait of a jester
Frans Verbeeck
Public domain
Changed to black and white

Invasive bamboo with rusty garden chair on a bank
of the River Arun in West Sussex, England.
Acabashi, own work
Creative Commons Attribution-ShareAlike
4.0 International licensing
Changed to black and white

Doctors and patient
Image generated by OpenAI's DALL-E within DALL-E,
facilitated by ChatGPT (GPT-4).
Cropped

Hand in action at hospital
Image generated by OpenAI's DALL-E within DALL-E,
facilitated by ChatGPT (GPT-4).
Cropped

Traveller in desert
Image generated by OpenAI's DALL-E
through ChatGPT (GPT-4)
Cropped

Surrealism, rimixography made with picsart
Aman Daharwal, own work
Creative Commons Attribution-Share Alike
3.0 Unported license
Cropped, changed to black and white, shadows

Washing a plate
Image generated by OpenAI's DALL-E within DALL-E, facilitated by ChatGPT (GPT-4).
Cropped

Old woman by trashcan
Image generated by OpenAI's DALL-E within DALL-E, facilitated by ChatGPT (GPT-4).
Cropped

Man on black mountain, hand in sky
Surrealism, rimixography made with picsart
Aman Daharwal, own work
Creative Commons Attribution-Share Alike
3.0 Unported license
Cropped

Human eye, anterior view
Rapidreflex, own work
Creative Commons Attribution-Share Alike
4.0 International license
Cropped, changed to black and white

Firebird
Image generated by OpenAI's DALL-E within Author, facilitated by ChatGPT (GPT-4).
Cropped, changed to black and white

The Sparrow
Image generated by OpenAI's DALL-E within the Virtual Poetry Critique by Professor Verse, facilitated by ChatGPT (GPT-4).
Cropped, changed to black and white